For my children and grandchildren and for my dear wife Terces,
who loves me and supports my rebellious proclivities.

Vigilance is the ability to witness thoughts, emotions and experiences arise without identification.
The vigilant watch their mind interpret what the senses perceive with equanimity, dwelling in the stillness that this practice elicits.

THE OBSERVANT MAN

VIGILANCE IN SPIRITUAL WARFARE

Matthew Engelhart

For Christmas 1971, my sister Libby brought home Ram Das' classic, Be Here Now. Not long after that, Yogananda's, The Autobiography of a Yogi came to my attention. I was in 10th grade at the time and became enamored with levitating saints and the concept of a guru, one who completely renounced self-interest to serve God and others. I remember being intrigued by the eastern notion that the soul is unborn, never having "not been". My mother, a confirmed atheist said, "I've got a mystic on my hands". Shortly after that, my best friend became a teacher of meditation; surely the mystery had found me. Over the next forty years, while raising families, creating businesses, making and losing fortunes, and getting divorced, I always applied myself with varying degrees of devotion to some kind of inner work, aspiring to unveil the Divine essence within.

There is a treasury of joy within you,
why do you keep begging door to door?
-Rumi

I studied with many traditions and teachers, and through the vehicles of meditation and plant medicine have experienced moments of the lifting of the veil, a taste of the higher (internal) worlds. I have kneeled before the magnificence of infinite love - an experience quite terrifying to the "I". I would gladly prostrate there in communion for eternity, but have had to return to this grosser (external) reality. Still, I find myself emboldened that little else matters than to reconnect with that heavenly sphere.

It was in my mid-fifties that my practice and commitment took a leap forward. At this time I encountered Gnosis, which teaches esoteric knowledge focused on the direct perception of God. Gnosticism, while ancient and at the source of most mystical traditions, was revived in the 20th century by Samuel Aun Weor. One revelation I received from this new laboratory (laboratus = work, orare = pray; labor of prayer) of Gnosis was the immense degree of hidden self-consideration that still occupied me. It was sobering to witness how my ego lurks in every corner of my being, and how the majority of my conversations were a solicitation for some kind of admiration.

One practice of Gnosis shares that the state of one's death is very similar to the state of one's dreams. In both cases we leave our body, in one case we get to come back. This seems to be quite a reasonable theory and is at least somewhat confirmable. In my dreams I am but a specter of vague memories with little identity, and my consciousness is drowned in a current of confusing psychological aggregates. Usually I am stalking around some foreign city unsure of what I am looking for. I surmised, "If my personality, the myself I often identify with, doesn't even survive the dream state, then how real can it be?" It shows that the normal waking self is temporary, only associated with the body. And in my case, my soul - my eternally present witness, is undeveloped. Lacking much agency, my dream life was not an inspiring experience, and I am quite sure the key to a more conscious death is a more conscious life. I found a new determination to regain the helm - to concentrate my full attention at will, without distraction. I have tasted heaven, the non-dual states, where there is perception (soul) without the obstacle of "I". But my day-to-day is still laced with the constructs/vices of the body/personality that appear to be at odds with the authentic self (soul) - that which can truly experience the Divine.

Recently my neighbor found me overloading his half empty bin with my excess recycling. He was perturbed and indignant that I presumed this was OK. Aspiring to be responsible and committed to workable community, I apologized, which restored the break in integrity. On further inspection, I saw that my regret was laced with pride for my humility and righteousness for the compassion I extended him. After all these years of "inner work" with the aggrandizement of Matthew still the operating principle, I find some comfort in the words of the Buddha:

At the end of the way is freedom. 'Til then, patience.

Imagine if I declared that I was going to train to be a neonatal heart surgeon. What would that commitment demand of me? Sacrifice, concentration, willpower, adoration, humility, patience, diligence, perseverance, discernment, honesty, vigilance, courage, persistence, innocence...and a mentor or community to hold me accountable for my commitment. For the far more ambitious pursuit of self-realization, I suggest the same holds true - and yet, it is largely a labor of elimination.

Your task is not to seek for love,
but merely to seek and find all the barriers within yourself
that you have built against it.
-Rumi

This book is an introduction to a rigorous training of purging your temple in order to host a superior experience. It may occur like a real grind. The ego incessantly propositions us, the soul, with the distraction of the separate, threatened self. Only by bringing the light of awareness to the distraction can we find liberty. The freedom that ensues when one can notice an envious thought arise without identifying with it, or quell a reactive emotional state before it displaces love and causes damage, is truly inspiring. I could write about dancing ecstatically under a full moon while singing to an animate, ensouled universe; these practices attract me as well. But learning to love discipline, virtue and taking dominion over our interior universe is what I've been called to share. Yes, there will be days of toil as one would expect in training for any Olympic task. Does mastery come any other way?

The price of freedom is eternal vigilance.
-Thomas Jefferson

My language is imbued with a martial urgency that some will find objectionable, but isn't this precarious 21st century life ripe for an overthrow inside and out? Doesn't the degeneration of our culture and the natural world demand a certain gravity? Our weak connection to our spiritual dimension has us trying to find fulfillment in things, sensations and circumstances which inspire a destructive "me"-centered existence. The masses await a savior or a new technology while others believe the natural course of evolution will reveal the remedy. Few see desire as the agent of our idolatry, and even fewer have the conviction to dissolve the liable elements within that would allow our humility to reign and the work of caring for each other and the earth to be our most authentic longing. This practice may seem self-indulgent. However, I truly believe establishing our attention in the eternal self transforms us into a pure instrument of service, and an activist for the reality of love.

The question then becomes not how long and narrow is the path, but how much do you treasure the Beloved and how done are you with being used by a construct that only causes suffering and has no inherent reality? This path begins prostrate before the mystery - humble, patient and following an ache for freedom. Thank you for considering the invitation.

All of humanity's problems stem from man's inability to sit quietly in a room alone.
-Blaise Pascal, Pensées

THE GREAT WORK

Who needs another spiritual book? I certainly do not. Most of the time I am on information overload. The masters have spoken and I have been quite content to be a student of scripture and the traditions. Do eternal truths and the perennial philosophy really need to be restated? Yet, with no intention of writing a book these pages have been delivered to me from the quietude of meditation and prayer. It feels right to share them knowing full well that the Word has been modified or corrupted by the ears of my defects. Despite these impurities, I am confident that something useful abides here.

The inscription at the entrance of the Oracle of Delphi says, "Man know Thyself and you shall know the Gods and the Universe." Similarly, the subject of this book is learning to navigate our inner life and thus have access to the kingdom of God within. This book is an aid for the reader to mindfully bear witness to spiritual warfare- the drama of light and dark forces within us, and is an invitation to throw oneself into the heat of battle.

The first premise of this book is that our attention, our consciousness, (I will use consciousness, essence, awareness and attention interchangeably) is contaminated and not under our dominion. This is quite verifiable. Close your eyes and follow your breath, put your attention on the air moving in and out of your nostrils. Try to maintain that focus. How long does it take before your will is usurped by another- a desire, a memory, impatience... The list goes on. In modern psychology this lack of continuity is probably considered normal, but in esotericism it is called "possessed." We do not possess our consciousness. Jesus tells us this in Luke 21:19, *"In your patience possess ye your souls."*

Perhaps the first step in being observant is to accept that we do not fully possess the gift of our awareness. Then we can begin to observe what does occupy us. In Mark chapter 5 when Jesus asks the possessed man (that would be us) who he is, the man answers, *"I am legion and we are many."* So who are the many? Meditate for any length of time and you will confirm these scriptures and see that the occupants of your asylum compete with each other for your attention; shame has its moment and then is ousted by pride which soon is upturned by lust. 84,000 different egos are mentioned in Buddhism and these are nearly infinite variants of the seven deadly sins of the Christian tradition. Add to this inner legion the conditioning of being born into a body, a family, a culture and our consciousness becomes fully identified as an "I." The soul gets overwhelmed by a personality built upon experiences- formulating likes, dislikes, habits, neuroses. We become overly identified with constructs like, "I am a patriot, an introvert, a foodie, a parent" and thus distance ourselves from our true nature. Bringing awareness and distinction to this veil of unconsciousness is the subject at hand. The Buddha brilliantly articulates the agenda of the imposter. He says that ignorance has two faces- craving and aversion. The ego's context is to seek pleasure/sensation and avoid pain. The infected soul chases impermanence causing suffering and distraction from its true identity. Paul describes our captivity in Romans 7:20, *"Now if I do what I do not want to do, it is no longer I who do it, but sin living in me."*

What is this essence that has been accosted? Consciousness is that which perceives- that which receives information and impressions. Consciousness, while it often identifies with the trappings of the "I," requires no past, no personality, no opinions, no desires. When unmodified, it is a state of peaceful alertness. Our consciousness drawn outward by the senses has lost the will to be internally present and perceive its true nature- our Being. The Being is also called the Intimate Christ, our Buddha Nature, our Innermost. The Being is the true us, the part of us that never fell and became identified with physicality, the senses, the "I." The Being is like an elite soldier who will not nor cannot leave us, the wounded essence, in the field. With infinite patience, eon upon eon, the Being waits for us to turn inward and partner with our inner master so it can return home to the higher kingdoms, to the cosmic God with the whole of itself. The Being is our coach and mentor. This relationship between the consciousness and the Being is articulated in the Bhagavad Gita as Arjuna (essence) and Krishna (Being). This book you are reading is another aid to our hero, the essence who against alarming odds can be free of sin, which are actions that miss the mark of love. Grace is our willingness to recognize and receive the wellspring of assistance from our Innermost. All that is missing is our attention, aimed at putting God above all things and defeating the forces invested in our selfishness and suffering.

The observant man brings his will to this siege and focuses his awareness to discern what is real and eternal from that which is false and a distraction. The Self has been obscured by a myriad of non-selves. Our opponent is masterful, his heavies, pride and lust are always lurking and setting snares. It is only through vigilance and humility that the observant man has a chance. First the particular imposter must be exposed. For example, recently I was being defensive, which is a form of pride. In meditation I saw that the defensiveness was covering up a feeling of helplessness. Upon further contemplation, I experienced my consciousness or attention as distinct from the agitation itself. I had become identified, intoxicated with the experience of defensive/helpless and had lost my inner witness. That which perceives had become identified with defensiveness but was not that. Once an ego has been distinguished as separate from myself, now a higher power has something to take aim at. I can pray for the pretender to be vanquished. Consider that in every moment the adversary wants to draw us out, anesthetize the witness- the perceiver, and have us identify with the thought, experience, desire and thus steal our power. The following aphorisms are crafted to hone our awareness, sharpen our lucidity and help us stand guard at our temple so no thieves may enter.

Recently I was boarding an airplane. As they called my section my consciousness was overtaken, I lost the plot (love) and my attention drifted to getting (desire) an overhead space for my bag. Eyes averted, I muscled into the line a bit oblivious. When I looked up, a few pairs of disappointed eyes lay upon me and I realized my "scarcity," my lack of presence, had now contaminated the space. I had demonstrated selfishness and I regressed to shame. My lack of courtesy was now the source of suffering for myself and others. Our trespasses are the source of discord, war, and spiritual amnesia. This is how we crucify the Intimate Christ (the experience of the Being) frequently for 30 pieces of silver (suitcase storage). Expand this scenario to 8 billion individuals and you have a fallen world- asleep to observing our process and the pain that ensues. Waking up can be agonizing. I am humbled by how enslaved to our sensorial life we have become. If our outer world is a reflection of our collective inner state, then nothing short of an internal rebellion will do. We tend to think the world's condition is caused by "the bad guys over there" and we miss the atrocities of our own internal board of directors. The Observant Man is my latest version of regime change. How much of the this veil can we lift? The bar is high. The foundation story of this epoch is that of a man so replete in Spirit that even when tortured to the edge of life, he could forgive his executioners. The kingdom of heaven is within, here and now. I think God wants what every father/mother wants- their children close to them. Is there a worthier pursuit?

My hope is that this book bolsters your resolve and has you take the battle to the territory of the enemy- your life. The "man" in the observant man is referring to a human being, mankind, all of us. It is stylistic. It is me and my current devotional process. Some may be critical of my repetitive use of "man" as the observant one. Why not another gender? I played with lots of alternatives - "Observant One," The Sage (like in the Tao Te Ching), alternating between Observant Man and Woman but concluded to keep true to how it has been delivered to me in silence. Man comes from the Sanskrit word "manas" meaning the perceiving mind. The word "man" has referred to all humanity up until recent times.

My apologies if this lands in some way offensive. Please consider that a desired outcome of being observant is to become identified only with our true identity- a blossoming soul intending to incarnate cognizant love. Identification with anything else- our choices, our bodies, our past, or our politics is ultimately an obstacle. That being said, personal substitutes for "man" are welcome.

Does anyone really want to talk about nurturing virtue? Who's interested in dissolving their "I?" I have concern that this book will be labeled too stoic and will be rejected by our overly permissive culture. On deeper inspection, these thoughts are simply an excuse intent on abating some future pain incase my writing is dismissed. What's authentic is that by being willing to sit quietly and receive these words, my awareness of my spark of a soul sits more resoundingly at the feet of my Being. This feels like some kind of progress on a journey that may dwarf geological time. There is comfort for me in knowing that there is no other curriculum. Bringing consciousness, a watchful witness, to the unconscious is and will always be our task. This is called the Great Work. The Intimate Christ is always speaking to us from within. *"Whomever is faithful unto me, incarnates me, recognizes me as their true self will have eternal life." -John 3:16."* To achieve this is explained in Mark 8:34, Jesus says, *"Whosoever will come after me, let him deny himself, and take up his cross, and follow me."* I propose these three revolutionary instructions are no small task: To deny oneself is to die mystically and eliminate our egos. We must purge ourselves of any identity other than our soul aspiring to realize our Being. In order to win this battle we will need all our energy and willpower. To take up our cross is to be continent with our sexual energy and transform it from animal desire into Divine adoration. This will unleash our Pentecostal Fire, our kundalini, cleanse our defects and build our solar body, our second birth. Finally we must crush the last remnants of our self-consideration in the service of others- follow me. These three jewels are the basis for all authentic mystical traditions that earnestly intend direct perception of the Divine.

I could report effusively on the flavor of an orange but to what end? Only by tasting an orange can we "know" an orange. In the same way these words can only point to or describe something indescribable. Transcendent wisdom can only be acquired through experience by creating the correlative conditions (ethics, faith, love of service, relaxation, energy conservation, concentration, humility, self-observation, discipline...) in one's consciousness. These pages were composed as an invitation to you to apply a new level of discernment to your psychology (psyche = soul, logia = study, study of soul). The ferocity of Jesus applying the whip to the money changers is what it is going to take to clean your temple so that your consciousness, your experience, can host the Beloved. On this journey it is important to remember that you are never alone. Listen to the silence in earnest, your Innermost is always there guiding you, reminding you of your Divine lineage. My hope is this book provokes an urgency in you to heroically take back your life from the imposter and wage love. This human opportunity is hallowed ground.

Whatever joy there is in this world all comes from desiring others to be happy [compassion], and whatever suffering there is in this world, all comes from desiring myself to be happy [lust]. But what need is there to say much more? The childish work for their own benefit, the Buddhas work for the benefit of others.
Just look at the difference between them!
-Shantideva

THE THREE JEWELS

Mother, Please rescue me,
I have fallen,
Charmed by vanities and appearances
I am occupied by a multitude,
I beseech you to sound the death toll,
Light the funeral pyre and
Incinerate these imposters,
Rise up in me through the merits of my heart and meet thy
husband in my crown,
I pray that I may hold thy intensity in the embrace of my beloved,
Such that in eternity I may praise the Beloved,
Let me put God above all things,
And serve His will to crush the remnants of the usurper,
Under the yoke of my devotion.

Artwork by Jon Marro

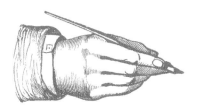

THE APHORISMS

A note about reading the aphorisms:
There is a mechanism (an ego) in many of us that intends to keep
our world view intact, keep us safe and maintain our status quo.
It will tend to assimilate new information through the filter of
agree/disagree, or true/false or believe/don't believe. If you are
satisfied with your spiritual progress, then this may be a good
strategy.
If not, I suggest that your perspective can be an obstacle.
Rather than measure these statements against your
existing mindset (the one giving you the life you have),
I suggest you sit with each aphorism in silence and see if these
words point in the direction of a new opportunity.
If not, move on.
The aphorisms are loosely sequential.
They can be read in order or randomly.

Artwork by Jon Marro

The observant man experiences a formidable opponent, the ego, that incessantly baits him to identify with the external objects of the world and forget his interior stillness. To deny the enemy, he must be vigilant and watch the usurper's enticements of craving and aversion while willfully staying seated at the inner altar's calm.

*Consider that we only experience our Being, our essence, and our egos. The Being is wisdom-
an experience of an indwelling stillness permeated with cognizant love. The essence is our attention,
it longs for agency and to know the Being, but is mostly distracted. The ego is the distraction- it
offers the past or future, it elicits craving and feeds on our subsequent suffering. The observant man is ever extracting his attention from this diversion by
remembering that he is the witness and not the victim of his interior life.*

*As the observant man contemplates his inner life,
he notices a myriad of egos vying simultaneously to
occupy his awareness. In a matter of moments- doubt,
arrogance and shame may fight one another to own his
attention. Their common cause is to distract his free
consciousness, the stillness from where he may watch them
feed.*

Artwork by Martin Schongauer, c. 1470-75

The observant man must apply energized attention to stay present, here and now in remembrance, all the while observing his inner legion's strategies to regain command.

The observant man's attention is all he really has. Where he places his only real possession is his highest priority.
He directs his worship power inward, intent on experiencing consciousness without the constraints of the "I."

To take dominion over his life, the observant man aspires to manage five aspects of his being- his thoughts, his speech, his beliefs, how he acts, and his attitude. These are the filters through which his life is perceived and thus they are the source of his experience.

The observant man must comprehend his defects as separate and distinct from his essence, that which perceives. Once distinguished, a higher power can be invoked to take aim at what he has recognized as clearly foreign entities.

The observant man makes a game of minding his mind. Whenever he notices he is reacting to the world, he remembers he lives at choice. He chooses his thoughts, emotions and actions, and anchors himself in gratitude.

He cannot serve two masters. To serve the Being is to root out desire, nurture virtue, and execute the instructions received in stillness. To serve the legion is to fulfill craving after endless craving accompanied by internal chaos. For the observant man, the examination of the source of all his motivations is key. He asks himself often, "Who is doing the choosing, whose will am I serving?"

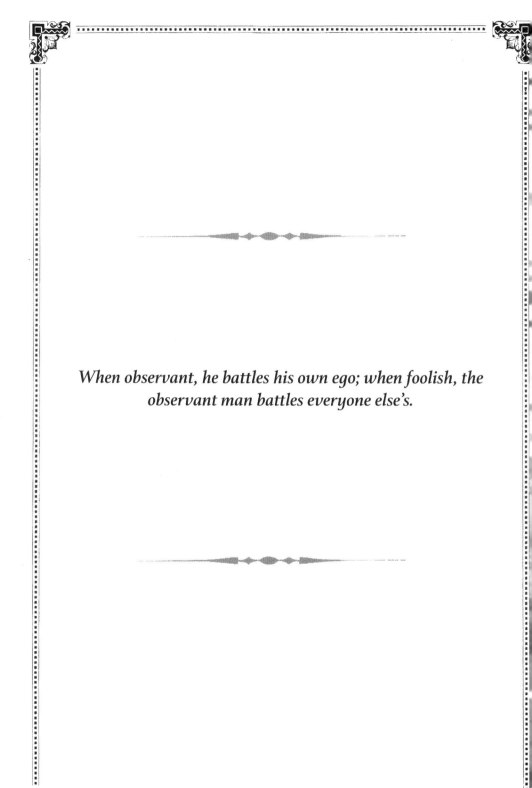

When observant, he battles his own ego; when foolish, the observant man battles everyone else's.

The observant man understands that the ego loves the critic's throne and often uses the premise, "something's missing" or "something's wrong" (with the world or with himself) to distract him from his true nature.
He is watchful for the temptation of brazen and disguised complaints ready to rob him of the indwelling presence of peace.

Artwork by Frank Ricchio

Cognizance is key to the observant man's freedom.
An example of this is, "I am noticing a thought arise that I
am not being appreciated by my friend."
An example of non-observance or identification is,
"I am not appreciated by my friend." When the
observant man sees a thought arise he is free, when he "is"
the thought, he is enslaved.

The observant man fights against the drift of cynicism and resignation by generating devotion to the inner work- the practice of being observant.

For the observant man, inner peace is paramount. Only in stillness can he be sure he hears his Being, unmodified by his inner legion.

The observant man attends to his attention.
He is dying to any other aspiration.
Taking sovereignty over his mind is his holy war,
his odyssey; this is his final quest.

For the observant man, every moment is a vigil, a meditation. He inwardly watches how his own inner adversary attempts to draw him out into the world of form and distract him from the stillness in his heart.

Artwork by Gustave Doré, c. 1890

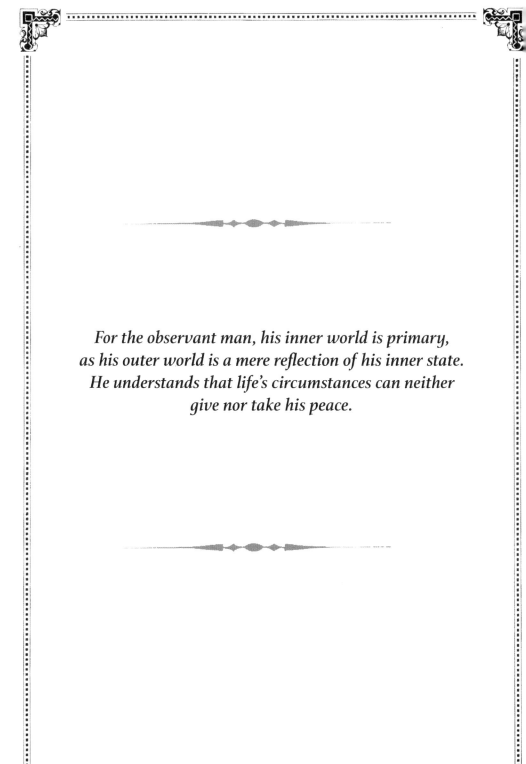

For the observant man, his inner world is primary,
as his outer world is a mere reflection of his inner state.
He understands that life's circumstances can neither
give nor take his peace.

The observant man considers his suffering a measure of his distraction. The breadth of his internal torment quantifies his lack of observance, his degree of identification.

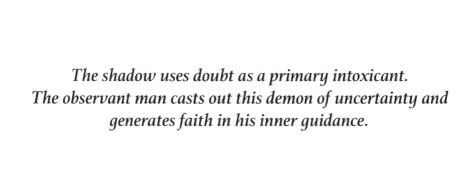

The shadow uses doubt as a primary intoxicant.
The observant man casts out this demon of uncertainty and
generates faith in his inner guidance.

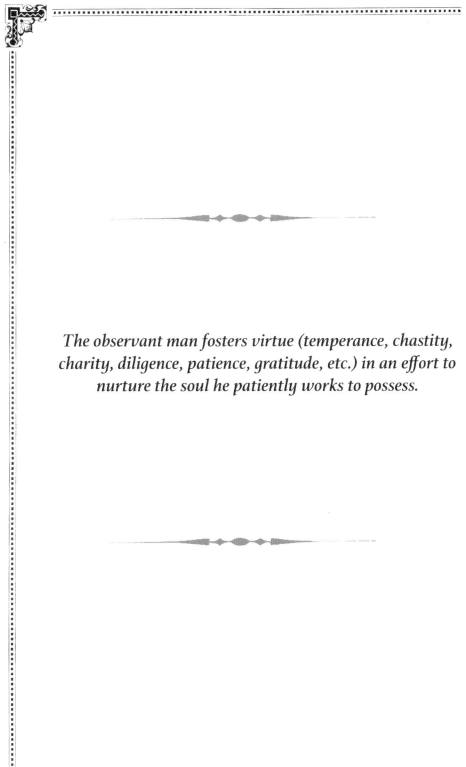

The observant man fosters virtue (temperance, chastity, charity, diligence, patience, gratitude, etc.) in an effort to nurture the soul he patiently works to possess.

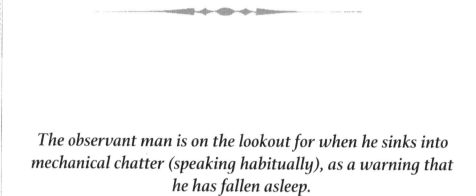

The observant man is on the lookout for when he sinks into mechanical chatter (speaking habitually), as a warning that he has fallen asleep.

While absolutely necessary, the observant man knows his own willpower will not be enough to slay his habitual defects. He will kneel often and call upon a higher authority to destroy the inner demons he isolates and comprehends as separate and distinct from his consciousness.

The observant man bows before his Being and implores his
Innermost to take full tenancy of his consciousness.
He sits quietly and watches his breath rise and fall, like
waves lapping at the shores of his inner ocean.
With patience the chatter ceases and a profound stillness
arises to occupy his experience.

The observant man stands guard, well aware that his senses fuel his amnesia. He understands these faculties tend to draw him out, away from his essence, overruling his ability to observe his inner process. To stay present in the throes of the battle, he often withdraws to the refuge of his breath.

The observant man vigilantly bears witness to what his attention, or worship power has become identified with. He corrects his course moment to moment throughout his day by remembering that he is the essence- a spark of free consciousness resisting anesthesia by desire.

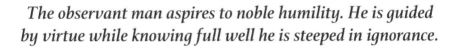

The observant man aspires to noble humility. He is guided by virtue while knowing full well he is steeped in ignorance.

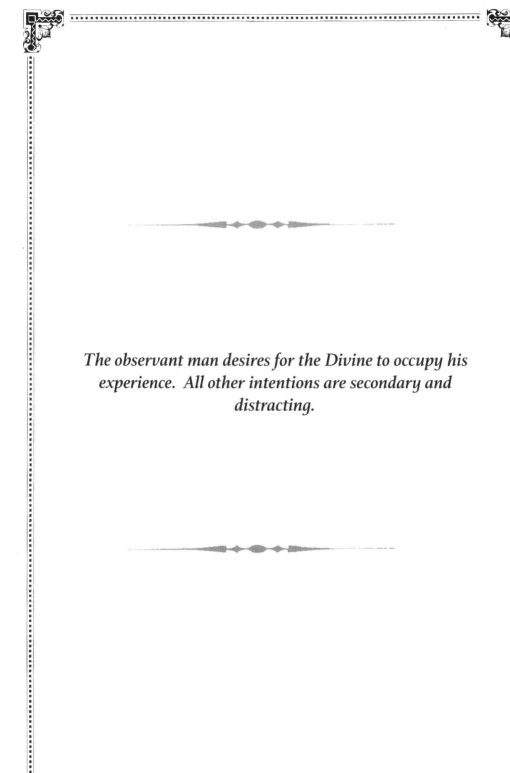

The observant man desires for the Divine to occupy his experience. All other intentions are secondary and distracting.

Artwork by Gustave Doré

Only actions impact his spiritual progress. Actions are thoughts, words, prayers, deeds, where and how he applies his attention. This inner work is not to appease or earn the favor of an absent Deity, but rather to make room to host a superior experience. The Beloved's tenancy within him is commensurate to the observant man's vacancy. There is no "I" in God.

The observant man imagines that God and he have the same intention- to share the same experience.

His vigilance approaches fanaticism. The observant man guards against anything that distracts him from lifting the veil to the experience of higher consciousness. Placing the inner work above all else is his first commandment.

The Being is an indwelling presence, and the observant man's ability to separate the wheat (love, virtue, wisdom, peace) from the chaff (ego, desire, pride, "I") in his internal experience is the battle.
With his will to be on watch, he fights to stay focused, present, and absorbed in stillness.
This is spiritual warfare.

The observant man aspires to be humble. He considers his judgements, assessments, and opinions a function of his identity, and thus temporal and meritless. When he notices himself overly invested in his perceptions, he gladly stands down and apologizes to anyone offended.

As the observant man strengthens his resolve to stay seated in love, the darkness intensifies its efforts; more insidious egos are called upon to dethrone him. This spiritual battle can only be won by his constant remembrance that he is not alone- that he has an ally which in fact is his true identity, his Being, his own intimate Deity.

The observant man is a request to be used by God.
He often prays for the revelation as to how to best be in the
service of love.

The observant man lives to serve God in others; he works to demonstrate love and ease suffering. Present to his devotion to the path and through the conscious effort of service, he voluntarily deprives his egos of their cravings and comforts.

*A thought appears- **I should call Jon**- he just watches it. Another thought surfaces- **maybe I'll write a post-apocalyptic novel**- and he takes the bait; he gets absorbed. The observant man identifies with the thought and it launches a cascade of fantasy and aberration. **Oops, where'd I go? I am the witness.** He watches another thought arise.*

The observant man knows that there are circumstances in life and there are his interpretations of those circumstances. He understands that it is in his "story" ("they're ignorant," "I hate maintenance," "I'm a victim.") of the conditions of life that his suffering arises. When he chooses life's circumstances without interpretation and gives up resisting "what is so," he is free.

The observant man knows the power of the word and its ability to elevate or diminish life. Intent on purity and clarity, he puts his words through a Socratic test before he speaks:

Is it true?
Is it kind?
Is it useful?
Is it necessary?

Recognizing the power of his word, the observant man keeps his promises, which includes a promise to be in communication when he can't keep his promise.

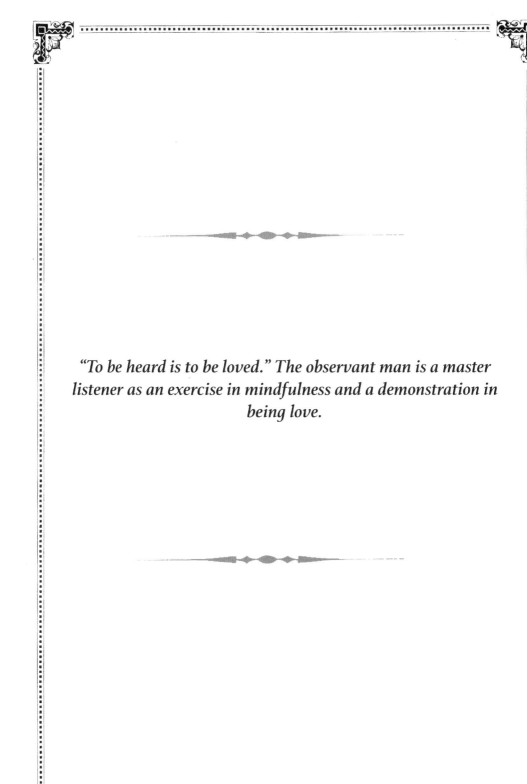

"To be heard is to be loved." The observant man is a master listener as an exercise in mindfulness and a demonstration in being love.

When his mind is quiet, adoration is his inherent experience. The observant man aspires to be done with pursuing love anywhere other than the temple of his heart.

The observant man's experience of peace with his finances, family of origin and intimate partnership are good litmus tests for how truly observant (anchored in life is an inside job) he is. These three highly triggering areas are ripe with opportunities to get identified. They call forth his ultimate attentiveness.

The observant man continually asks and answers these three questions (with frequent revision):

Who is having this experience?
The consciousness, the essence, a calm abiding witness.

Where is this experience located?
In the abode of my heart; here, now, present.

What am I doing?
Incarnating Love, realizing my Being, dying to the will of God, taking possession of my soul.

As he develops a more acute awareness of his behavior, the observant man is confronted by how often his words are a solicitation of love and admiration from others.

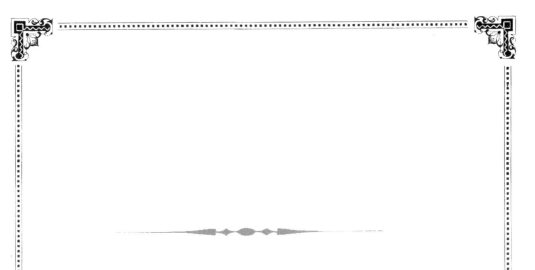

When the observant man is humble, he looks for who to serve. When he is prideful, he looks for who can take notice.

Karma, "As you sow, so shall you reap," is understood by the observant man as the law. He humbly accepts his adversities as payments in kind for past infractions of ignorance.

The observant man takes ownership of every unpleasant circumstance in his life. He is responsible for these karmic aggregates, the great law mirroring back his past actions. Every blessing in his life is of and from his Creator. His life is praise.

If he is happy it is because he remembers he is on a path; he is a grateful soul incarnating his Being.
If he is sad it is because separation is bitter and his soul longs to realize its Divine lineage. To the observant man all other explanations or propositions obscure this truth.

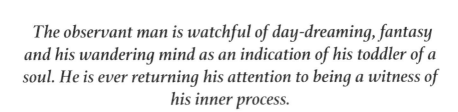

The observant man is watchful of day-dreaming, fantasy and his wandering mind as an indication of his toddler of a soul. He is ever returning his attention to being a witness of his inner process.

The observant man loves playing "Sentry of the Temple." Watchfulness is his active meditation. The ego dissolves into infinitely subtler forms of lust, pride, judgement, indolence, etc. He stands guard observing these enticing vermin and their primary offering, which is an insatiable ache for more.

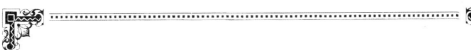

As the observant man fiercely protects his chastity, the darkness conspires to have him spill his sexual energy and dim his will which lights the path.

With craving in opposition to his freedom, sexuality is the observant man's ultimate trainer. On guard to lust's persistence that he spill his seed, he transforms the urge to release into adoration of the Beloved. With pranayama he sublimates his sexual serpentine fire upward, anointing his crown and nurturing the true ecstatic.

Our unconscious tendency to be steeped in desire, enamored with things and identified with our personality is the hypnotic state of most human beings. This understanding is the observant man's source of compassion, forgiveness and pity for himself and humanity.

The observant man sees pride, especially spiritual pride as his nemesis. Every time he notices his arrogance concealing itself as a passionate solicitation of another into his current version of "the truth," he remembers he is asleep. He must continually relinquish any need to proselytize.

Humility is the beginning of wisdom. On his knees the observant man feels his arrogance deflate into the charm of self-imposed submission.

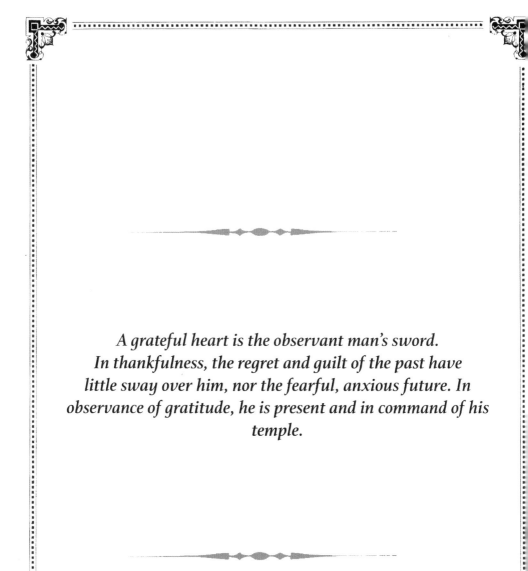

*A grateful heart is the observant man's sword.
In thankfulness, the regret and guilt of the past have
little sway over him, nor the fearful, anxious future. In
observance of gratitude, he is present and in command of his
temple.*

The observant man is a revisionist; he is always willing to die or divest in his current state of "truth" or consciousness, such that he can be reborn into the next mystery.

When a defect dies, a virtue is born. To nurture a character of goodness (being in the service of love for others) is the continuous work of the observant man.

At the day's end, the observant man studies where he lost his inner compass and fell prey to his defects. He recalls which ego displaced his power to stand guard, and he aspires to comprehend the ego as an alien who stands in as his consciousness.

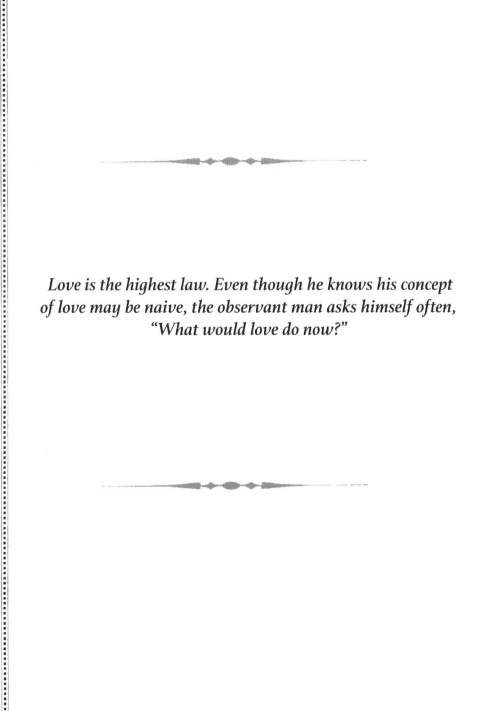

Love is the highest law. Even though he knows his concept of love may be naive, the observant man asks himself often, "What would love do now?"

Knowing only the ego can be humiliated, the observant man is happy to apologize and take responsibility for what others perceive as an infraction. Humility is the mainstay of his devotion.

The observant man owns that he is asleep as a humble reminder that his consciousness, his experience of God, is infantile.

What are the symptoms of hypnosis? Suffering, desire, agitation, anxiety, unwanted emotions, pride, gluttony, lust, anger, impatience, greed, stinginess, distrust, avoidance...and the list goes on. Present to the enormity of the task, the observant man cultivates patience and the will to remain a witness, not a victim of his interior landscape.

The observant man has great compassion for the human condition, and for all the essences (budding souls) imprisoned in the modifications of the ego. He has no such feelings for the usurper itself. It is a psychological parasite- the source of suffering, an opponent to God, and worthy of his conviction to eliminate it.

The observant man is wary of the trap of expectations and how he sets himself up for disappointment. He favors transparency about his preferences; he makes requests and is grateful for whatever he receives.

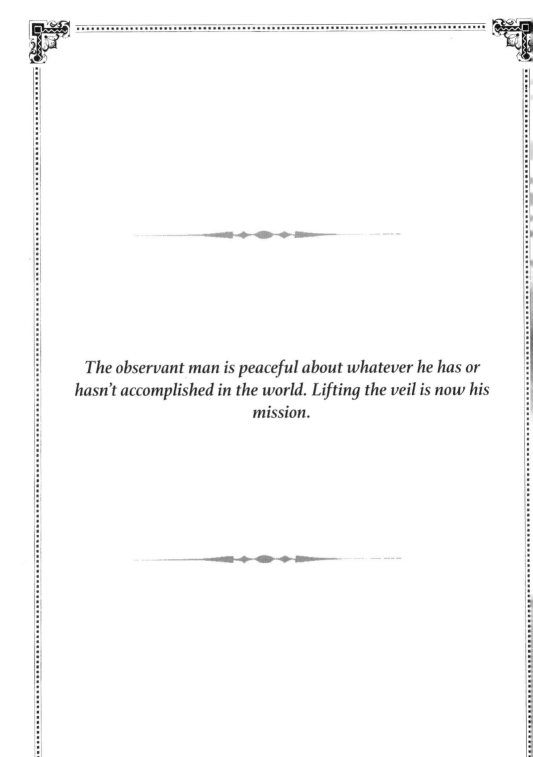

The observant man is peaceful about whatever he has or hasn't accomplished in the world. Lifting the veil is now his mission.

Love is the sum of all wisdom. The observant man demonstrates the degree of love in his heart in his service to others. Through sacrifice he defeats his own self-consideration.

Consciousness is that which perceives. He is not his thoughts, feelings, or urges, but that which receives these impressions. Most of what he perceives is in error curated by the enemy. When the observant man willfully directs his attention to just observe his internal weather and let it pass through his experience, he is free.

To be observant is to bear witness to one's interior universe. The observant man watches his thoughts, feelings, and fancies wax and wane with dispassion. He must patiently endure the chaos of competing utterances and the ensuing opacity until the mind settles into a clear experience of consciousness, serenely aware of itself.

The observant man is in the world but requires nothing of it. Whatever or whomever there is before him is what there is to attend to. Here and now is where love is served.

Ecclesiastes 1:14, I have seen everything that is done under the sun and behold, all is vanity and striving after wind.

Inspired by Solomon, the observant man knows that most human activity is driven by grosser or subtler forms of vanity. He is on guard for the ego as it relentlessly entices him to inflate his self-importance.

The observant man suspects he has a mountain of karma (cause and effect) that he has yet to reap. To prevent the accumulation of more effect, he takes the Golden Rule, "Do unto others as you would have them do unto you" very seriously. He looks for opportunities to serve and delight others, demonstrate love, ease suffering and perhaps rectify the consequences of his past errors descending onto his life.

The observant man is the warrior-will devoted to serving his king, the Being. He never underestimates the myriad of forces that conspire to derail his liberation and land him in the abyss. In the tempest of the usurper's distractions, he marshals his attention to remain a witness and unidentified with that which he perceives. He prays for clarity on how best to oblige his sovereign.

In his internal experience, the observant man is present to a perceiver distinct from that which is perceived. When his attention crosses the line from witnessing an experience to being captured by what his senses are receiving, the perceiver (soul) is lost in identification. He is then at the whim of his chaotic mind, urges and emotions. To have possession of his soul is to have command of his internal witness.

The observant man knows his experience of life is merely his response to his own impressions of existence. But his impressions have no inherent reality ; they are superficial misperceptions. So his responses to these errors of perception also have no reality. He makes up what is true and is often agitated by what he makes his truth mean. He grants compassion to himself and to all his relations for this trap of ignorance in which we all dwell.

If not present to the internal battle for his consciousness, the observant man must assume he is possessed or asleep. He knows the enemy is a shapeshifter concealing itself in ever subtler aspects of his personality.

If the observant man is bored, he is asleep and not present. Boredom is the enemy's craving for a sensation and its aversion to the here and now. He used to medicate his weariness with media and entertainment. Now, more and more he chooses to meditate and patiently squirm with the critters in his asylum, waiting to drop into the treasury of quietude below their agitation.

The observant man understands and guards against entropy- the tendency of his consciousness to drift towards comfort, the status quo and the collective malaise. Diligence means continuity of practice.

The observant man does not avoid the upsets or stormy emotional weather of others. He knows they are a practice in being present and compassionate, but not identified. His mantra is, "their upset is my meditation."

The observant man brings forth ongoing regeneration to his life through sacrifice, death and birth:

Sacrifice- Abstain, starve the ego of its desire and need to feed itself. Serve others.

Death- Comprehend the defect, ego, vice as a foreign entity (distinct from his consciousness and a source of suffering) and pray to a higher power to destroy it.

Birth- Nurture or practice a virtue in the new psychological space.

The observant man suspects that his will to harness his attention, the virtues his budding soul has incarnated, and his imprisoning egos are all that survive bodily death. He divests in his personality, assured that what time can dissolve lacks reality.

With nothing to defend or protect except his soul from distraction, the observant man is transparent about the defects of his very temporary personality. He happily laughs about his inner demons and their antics. He is humbled by the power of his identity to overwhelm and anesthetize his inner witness.

The observant man examines how easily he hypnotically slips into identification. "I am a foodie, a Dylan fan, a rebel, an organic farmer..." These are bankrupt. He remembers that in fact, he is a spark of free consciousness trapped inside an identity that resists mystical death with the vigor of a drowning man.

The observant man has little tolerance for small talk. In every conversation he takes a risk. He asks the questions that expose the ego and identify the distraction causing the suffering (complaint, limitation, an unwanted emotional experience.) His dialogues are a reminder that we live at choice, that our attention is all we own and he invites us to worship at the altar of our interior Deity.

The observant man scrutinizes his ambition and how it continually dissolves into subtle aspirations that bolster his personality and ultimate disappointment. The one conscious desire he allows himself is to know the Beloved. Still, even this the enemy can abduct through spiritual pride for its own purposes.

The observant man divests in his persona so that his true identity, the Being, can slowly arise in his experience.
To dissolve the distraction of his personality, his practice is to:
Abstain- he observes the desire or ego but doesn't identify with it.
Be silent- he speaks only when it is kind, true, necessary, useful.
Die- he is frugal with his opinions and projections as he remembers he is steeped in ignorance. He humbly lives in the "I don't know."

The intoxication of worldly success must be treated with caution. The observant man never assumes that he has graduated from the distorting influence of money or admiration.

The observant man asks for help every day. Humbled by the magnitude of this task he finds solace on his knees, as he listens for guidance.

For the observant man, prayer is life. Prostrate before his Divine Mother, pledging his allegiance and petitioning for assistance, the enemy finds little purchase.

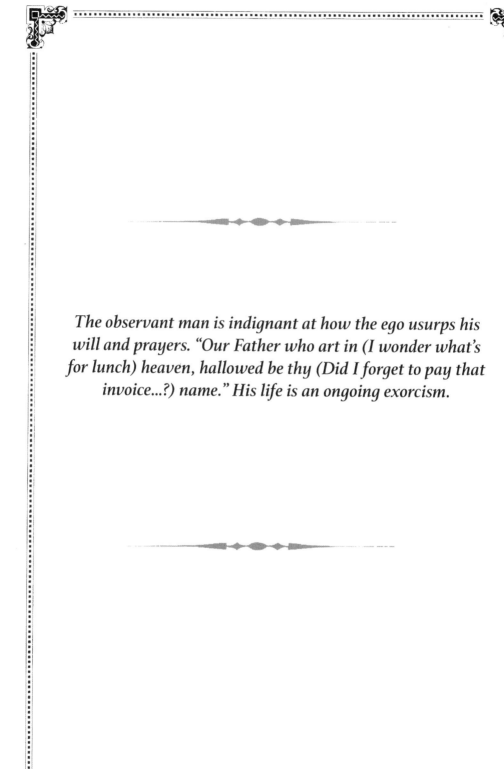

The observant man is indignant at how the ego usurps his will and prayers. "Our Father who art in (I wonder what's for lunch) heaven, hallowed be thy (Did I forget to pay that invoice...?) name." His life is an ongoing exorcism.

Since humiliation is the territory of the ego, the observant man makes big, bold requests of others without concern. Hearing "no" from those he petitions and the demons it provokes within him are more grist for his mill of comprehension.

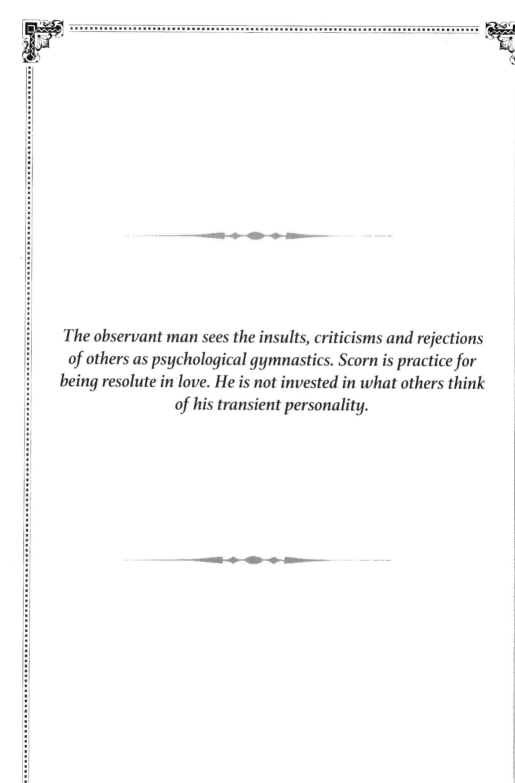

The observant man sees the insults, criticisms and rejections of others as psychological gymnastics. Scorn is practice for being resolute in love. He is not invested in what others think of his transient personality.

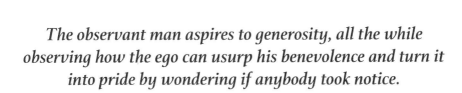

The observant man aspires to generosity, all the while observing how the ego can usurp his benevolence and turn it into pride by wondering if anybody took notice.

The observant man exercises pity and compassion for himself, his brethren, the human condition and the depth of our unconsciousness. "Forgive us Father for we know not what we do," is his mantra.

*Betrayal is part of the training for the observant man.
The exhibition of disloyalty by a trusted loved one provokes
deeply entrenched egos for him to comprehend and eliminate.
The remedy is forgiveness, recognizing how formidable the
enemy is, and how easily we all go unconscious.*

The observant man understands that, "Love thy enemy" means to appreciate the service this adversary plays in his development. First, he exercises compassion for the soul trapped in the imprisoning vices of the antagonist. Next, he examines the demons (anger, violence, hate) that this foe elicits within him. With these egos now exposed, he has the opportunity to comprehend them and pray for their eradication.

Whether partnered or not, the observant man aspires to be continent with his sexual energy. He retains and directs this inner fire to fuel his will to be observant and anoint his spiritual progression.

Scientific chastity means illuminating sexual emotion with Divine adoration, and retaining the charged energy field created in physical intimacy for worship. This means copulation with a promised partner while refraining from orgasm. This requires olympic level attentiveness from the observant man. Sexual priesthood is the ultimate practice in "deny thy ego self."

For the observant man, his intimate partner is his 24/7 emotional/spiritual mirror; she provides training in attentiveness. He plays the game of being 100% responsible for the condition of the relationship (how much love, harmony and support are present.) This is not the truth, but the only place to powerfully stand. He uses every opportunity to apologize for any lack of thoughtfulness as a practice in humility. He has preferences, he makes requests, and is grateful for whatever he receives. He acknowledges his partner frequently for training him in love without conditions. He attends to his beloved as a practice in egoic death and the dissolution of the "I."

Through meditation practice the charm of matter dims.
As the observant man is incrementally absorbed in silence,
the "I" is relieved of its duty. Gradually his self interest fades
and love has a vehicle to act upon the world.

*Sins are actions that "miss the mark" of love,
(the word comes from a Greek archery term.) To sin is to
apply one's attention to feeding an ego or desire.
The observant man is a sinner; he misses the mark trying
to find love and fulfillment in things, people, sensations.
Wanting and the experience of love are incompatible. Love
is whole and complete and wants nothing for itself but to
express love, serve love, and inspire love.*

The observant man is amused by how he can over-emphasize his inner warrior at the expense of other archetypes or qualities of his Being. He reminds himself that at the heated battle's end, it is an innocent child that enters the kingdom.

The observant man knows that to speak to superior beings,
his own tongue must have lost the power to wound.
Gossiping, speaking or listening to diminishing words about
another is an insidious obstacle to his awakening.

To be honorable and impeccable with one's words and deeds is part of attentiveness. Additionally, the observant man aspires to be pristine with his internal conversations.
In the privacy of his heart, can he also be gracious towards all his relations?

The observant man must remember to balance his warrior/ father/mind with his nurturer/mother/heart. He is on the watch for an absence of sacrifice, compassion and vigilance. He knows that the ego of fanaticism is born of extremities.

The observant man follows this thread:

How did I suffer today?
(He looks for an emotional experience he didn't enjoy)
Example- Impatience.

What attachment caused the suffering?
Ex.- Getting through his to-do list.

What desire created the attachment?
Ex.- To know himself as accomplished or powerful.

What is the ignorance that birthed the desire?
Ex.- I am not enough, I am my accomplishments.
Fulfillment comes from outside.

The observant man's friends tell him he used to be more fun. Sometimes his love for God and his rigor to stay pure translates as stoic and anti-social. Sometimes he gets caught by an ego called, "others are going to distract me." Sometimes he just needs to lighten up and laugh at his insatiable longing to go home.

Pridefully thinking he'd extinguished envy, the observant man found subtler versions of resentment lurking in the catacombs of his mind- an unwillingness to celebrate the success of others and even more revolting, a wish for their failure. This discovery reminds him that his temple is still defiled, and that a floor is scrubbed on one's knees.

To the observant man, egoic death is terrifying, but still preferable to the stagnation of serving the unconscious desires of his polluted personality. He aspires to choose conscious effort and voluntary suffering. He concentrates on remaining an unidentified witness as he denies the demands of the enemy. Dissolving the "I" is his greatest ambition.

Through the senses, the ignorance of mankind and the acts of this fallen world vie for his attention; there are countless political and social outrages to capture his awareness. Through the subtler senses of intuition and inspiration, the Beloved calls. The observant man resists the seduction of "the outer bait" and hones his listening on the silence.

The observant man is generous, not to gain the admiration of others or to medicate his own guilt or self-loathing but to demonstrate to himself that his real treasure and security are in heaven- his internal world.

The observant man vigilantly examines his addictions and neuroses of distraction. His relationship to his phone, social media, e-mail and entertainment choices can be instruments of avoidance from his inner battle. Without facing and defeating his inner demons, he will never know the peace that far surpasses the temporary medication these diversions provide.

The observant man doesn't choose this or that, he chooses to live in the freedom of choice. On the path there are countless courses of action, and once chosen, he must own them and continue the battle without the constraints of doubt. To live as a warrior is to boldly choose.

The observant man is astute to his gluttonous tendencies. Not just with food but information, the news, conspiracy theories, entertainment, shopping, a new gizmo... He regularly denies his gluttony an extra helping, knowing the craving is never extinguished by fulfilling the desire.

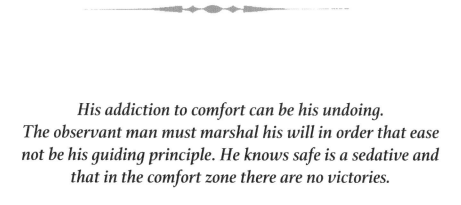

His addiction to comfort can be his undoing.
The observant man must marshal his will in order that ease
not be his guiding principle. He knows safe is a sedative and
that in the comfort zone there are no victories.

As our permissive, promiscuous, immediate gratification culture elicits its temptations on the observant man, he plays the game of penance. He is always abstaining from some enticement to provoke a skirmish with the enemy.

How does the observant man stay beholden to the path?

Adoration- loving and being moved by God (the multi-unity of beings that conspire for his liberation.)

Concentration- honing his awareness inwardly on the Being.

Willpower- preserving and marshaling his life force to be present, here and now, in the service of love.

Patience- remembering that the path is a long haul and that the enemy, not wanting to die, will use any means to discourage and distract him.

Humility- knowing the "I" he experiences as self is fallen and steeped in ignorance. He petitions God for assistance.

For the observant man, meditation is as integral to life as eating. When his mind is still and present, the indwelling presence of love fills his experience. "Give us this day our daily bread," is a request for a taste of the Lord's experience to be infused with his own.

In meditation, the observant man momentarily touches that spark of free, still, unmodified consciousness. This is his true identity. Identifying as anything else- Gnostic, male, successful, American, having tattoos, an organic farmer...is temporal and ultimately a source of suffering. He remembers this stillness while nurturing a personality of virtue and rejecting the vices that possess him.
This is the life of a spiritual warrior.

In Matthew 8:22, "Follow me and let the dead bury the dead," Jesus makes clear the priority of listening to the Intimate Christ. The life of the observant man is this inner work- the possessing of his soul (recovering his awareness from the usurper,) so the Father's experience (love and wisdom) may incarnate in his consciousness.

The observant man uses lucidity in his dreams to gauge his progress. He is encouraged if observance, his ability to bear witness to his experience, penetrates his dream state.

Pierre-Narcisse Guérin - Morpheus and Iris c. 1811

The Buddhists call this world of tears, Samsara. The observant man used to be distracted trying to save the planet from the defilers. He now knows the real enemy and follows it closely. From suffering to attachment, from attachment to desire, from desire to a separation from God. Our interior landscape is the source of our tears and this is where humanity will be redeemed.

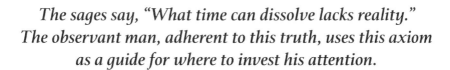

The sages say, "What time can dissolve lacks reality."
The observant man, adherent to this truth, uses this axiom
as a guide for where to invest his attention.

The wisdom keepers of Hindustan declare that the mind, prana (our vital energy or Chi) and the semen (the sexual energy) are correlative. To have dominion over one grants control of the others. For the observant man, meditation, pranayama (yogic breath work,) and the sublimation of the sexual energy are foundational practices to undertake the "Great Work."

If the observant man indulges in regret, it is for not using his life more wisely and being lazy about the inner work.

How does the observant man measure his spiritual progress? How can he quantify his comprehension, his experience of the indwelling Deity? By the self/others index. How much of his attention is on placating the appetites of the "I" and how much on serving others? The results are often disparaging, but this kind of daily inventory alerts him to the immensity of the work at hand, and the need to double down on defeating his self-consideration.

Extracting the "I" is a daunting task. ("Narrow is the path and straight is the gate.") The observant man is in for the long haul, and patience is his constant, steady refuge.

What does he really need? Food, water, warmth, a quiet place to pray, a few dear relations, the books and music of the masters, encounters with the natural world. Much beyond these things, "things" are a distraction. The observant man wishes he had invested more in cultivating his inner heavens and less in chasing outer sensations.

Sometimes the observant man feels cocky and un-mess-with-able, like nothing could seduce him to fall. When he comes to his senses and recovers from this delusion, he humbly kneels and prays to be delivered from such arrogance.

Often an ego convinces the observant man to repeat an old failed experiment- that is, to try to find fulfillment by satisfying his desires. He discovers suffering at three levels (for example, wanting a house):

Craving the thing- satisfaction in future, not now.
Maintaining the thing- the responsibility of the thing itself becomes a burden, better to be free of mortgage, taxes, maintenance.
Losing the thing- impermanence; when we invest in the temporary, we suffer when having to let it go.

He chooses to seek his internal treasury and practices being fulfilled and present here and now. He is weary of begging door to door.

The shadow uses inferior emotions to maintain its tenancy within him. When observant, he can deny these enslaving reactive states. Refraining from these triggers is a victory for the observant man, in which the spoils are a deeper experience of the internal witness.

*For the observant man, his faith begins with an experiment
as he humbly asks his Being to occupy him in meditation.
With patience, his experiment becomes the experience of
peace of the Intimate, his ally pledged to his awakening.*

"For God so loved the world, that he gave his only begotten son, that whoever is faithful unto him should not perish, but have everlasting life." John 3:16

The observant man listens to the historical Jesus speaking to him from within as the Intimate Christ. Being faithful unto him is humbly submitting to a rigorous life of mystical death (Sanctity), sexual alchemy (Chastity), service (Charity) and meditation.

The observant man is grateful for those who have demonstrated that finding fulfillment in the external world is folly. Countless are those who have achieved greatness in art, beauty, charity, wealth, knowledge, and yet these accomplishments could not penetrate their internal hell realms. Instead, they were left languishing in torment. The observant man beams with gratitude for the practice of surrendering again and again to two great truths, "Life is an inside job," and "Love is an indwelling presence."

His consciousness is that which perceives, that which receives impressions, thoughts, emotions, urges. When isolated through meditation and withdrawn from the senses, the observant man becomes aware of his awareness. It is then that he experiences his true nature- a watchful, unconstrained stillness.

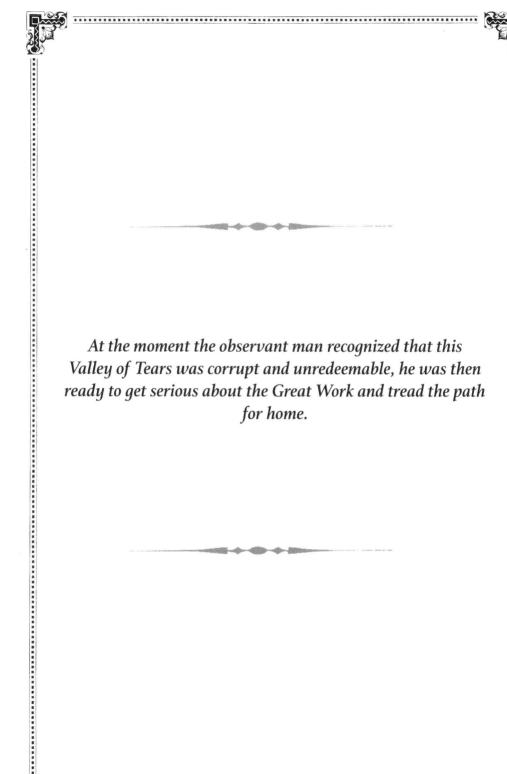

At the moment the observant man recognized that this Valley of Tears was corrupt and unredeemable, he was then ready to get serious about the Great Work and tread the path for home.

Buddhism guides him with the eight worldly concerns:

1. Gift (stuff)
2. No Gift (not enough stuff)
3. Comfort
4. Discomfort
5. Fame
6. No Fame
7. Praise
8. Criticism

*This is what binds him. This is what has him
identified with the "I" at the expense of eternal life.
Renunciation requires that every possible particle of his
attention is placed internally. Only through
rigorous psychological work, (meditation, self-
observation, self-remembrance) and sacrifice for others
fueled by the preserved sexual energy does he have a chance.
This is his path.*

As the observant man contemplates his death, he suspects he will have to answer for all his acts, non-acts, and every moment he put something above the Great Work. He prays for mercy, is genuinely repentant, and demonstrates his love of God by dying again and again to all other distractions.

As he reviews the different mindsets he has adapted throughout his life- Hinduism, raw food, Reaganism, he sees that belief is fickle. His faith is demonstrated by what occupies him. The observant man knows to what he grants his attention is to what he is most loyal. His devotion to God is not demonstrated by a particular belief, but by how willing he is to continually die to his pride and serve others.

To love is to know Me. The act itself of loving is indeed the experience of really knowing Me, for I am Love.
-Bhagavad Gita

"Being right," the pride of having one's opinion, thought or view trump another's is an insidious addiction of humanity. When the observant man notices he is in the trap of righteousness, lobbying for his position to bolster an ego at the expense of love's indwelling presence, he immediately bows out and apologizes for being overtaken.

To ward off his inherent arrogance and his propensity to say "I know," the observant man consciously practices the mantra, "I don't know." He abstains from jumping into conversations to feed a prideful ego and relishes dwelling in silence and humility.

Freedom arises in his experience as "wanting" uses him less. The observant man is amused by how temporary the gratification of a desire is, and finds it satisfying to build his muscle in abstaining from a persistent craving.

When the observant man notices he is chasing gratification, he stops, takes a deep breath, and notices the emotional state of the craving. He then declares inwardly or out loud, "If I had that, then I'd be happy." In this way, he humorously calls out the insatiability of the enemy.

*The word **obedience** grates on the ears of this modern, permissive culture as if submission was optional. The observant man sees that he is always in service to a will of some kind. More often than not, he is complicit to craving a sensation or avoiding one.*

"Realizing the truth of your True Self Within (Atma) is your principal weapon for eradicating desire. Self-realization is the true spiritual knowledge. This level of knowing is beyond all your lower qualities, no matter how fine, including your mind and even your intellect. Let your very highest Self, your true nature, rule. Control your self, with your Self."

-Bhagavad Gita

He who forgives little, loves little. The observant man nurtures compassion for the trap in which we all dwell, and is present to how easily he goes unconscious. He aspires to grant everyone, "Forgive us our trespasses, as we forgive those who have trespassed against us."

Enough is enough. Another day goes by, trapped in a craving personality desperate to find fulfillment in matter. Heaven is achieved by those that are done-done. It is time the observant man conquers his laziness and get to the task. This Great Work is an ally of efforts between a longing soul and a benevolent Deity.

Effort means expending energy. The observant man has squandered much vitality, either chasing a sensation or avoiding one. Now, he aspires to use his life force to create the necessary conditions in his consciousness (ethics, love of service, relaxation, conservation of energy, concentration, self-observation, humility, faith......) for the realization of the Intimate to arise.

The observant man identifies three traitors internally: Judas- desire, Pilate- the mind (justification and rationalization,) and Caiaphas- laziness and hypocrisy. To vanquish these enemies requires the most rigorous discernment and prayers for assistance. Their agenda is to negate the Intimate Christ and create spiritual amnesia.

Putting aside beliefs, doctrine and dogma, what are the facts? What can the observant man actually validate as true by his experience?

1. I am a perceiving separate self, an "I" that identifies with this body. There is "me," and there is "other than me."

2. The experience of this separate self is erratic, I have little dominion over my consciousness; thoughts, emotions, cravings, fears, fantasies and daydreams vie for my attention.

3. My experience is mostly fixed in the past or future; I am rarely present or at peace.

4. When I withdraw my senses from the external world and meditate, I experience a witness that abides outside of this drama of the separate self. The qualities of this inner watcher are stillness, peace, and cognizant love.

5. Through a meditation practice, self-observation and self-remembrance, I can strengthen the experience of this inner witness and thus displace the experience of the anxious ridden "I."

While scriptures and the traditions (how the scriptures have been lived) are foundational guides to his practice, it is in his own internal laboratory (laboratus = work, orare = pray, labor of prayer) that the truth is tested and confirmed.

The observant man has identified three formidable demons: self-pity, self-love (being enamored with one's personality,) and self-consideration (being better than others or putting one's wants and needs above others.) He watches for these assassins throughout the day, and in meditation, prays for their eradication.

We can rise to the summits of light only on the steps of love and sacrifice.

-Samael Aun Weor

Regardless of his beliefs, his faith is demonstrated by what he grants his attention to. His actions prove his faith. To be faithful in a marriage requires continuity in thought and deed, to be faithful to God the same. The observant man's ongoing willingness to exorcise his pride and serve others illuminates his devotion.

The observant man's first gift to God is ethics- virtuous impeccability with his thoughts, deeds and word. His next offering is to withdraw from the senses and ask the Beloved to take full tenancy. Absorbed in stillness, he is available to receive instructions without corruption.

Anyone who blasphemes against the Son of Man will be for-given, but anyone who blasphemes against the Holy Spirit will not be forgiven, either in this age or in the age to come."
Matthew 12:32

The observant man is cognizant that his sexual energy, a gift of the Holy Spirit, is the fuel for his spiritual progression- his ascent of Jacob's Ladder. When he reviews the volume of time spent possessed by carnal desire, fantasy, and his wanton misuse of his sexual energy (spilling his seed,) he is deeply regretful and ashamed. He has rejected the gift and blasphemed the Holy Spirit and for this he must pay the full karmic debt (not forgiven.) He lingers on this bitter pill so as to galvanize the road of scientific chastity before him.

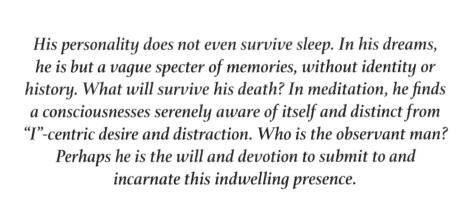

*His personality does not even survive sleep. In his dreams,
he is but a vague specter of memories, without identity or
history. What will survive his death? In meditation, he finds
a consciousnesses serenely aware of itself and distinct from
"I"-centric desire and distraction. Who is the observant man?
Perhaps he is the will and devotion to submit to and
incarnate this indwelling presence.*

1 Corinthians 13:4-5, "Love is patient, love is kind. It does not envy, it does not boast, it is not proud. It does not dishonor others, it is not self-seeking, it is not easily angered, it keeps no record of wrongs."

Upon reading Paul, the observant man understands that his day to day experience of love is contaminated. Through the filter of his legion, he knows desire, attachment, expectations and dependency disguised as adoration. He relishes the scarce encounters with his Being and with it, a love that dispels any sense of a solitary self.

Ethics is the preparation for serenity, for how can he know peace while participating in harmful behavior? Serenity is preparation for wisdom, for how can he receive a clear perception of the truth with the instrument of a chaotic mind? Stillness is the innate quality of the soul when liberated from the modification of his defects; from this purchase, the observant man can hunt egos and pierce the mysteries.

The observant man distinguishes anger from righteous indignation. The former is personal, habitual, familiar and leaves him exhausted, feeling out of control and completely identified- without a witness. The latter is called upon- consciously generated to make a point, to get a stubborn ego's attention. It is spontaneous, impersonal, and the energy of righteous indignation dissipates into the next moment. He imagines a child walking out into traffic and having to scream to get their attention- righteous indignation is like that.

With greater frequency, the observant man experiences consciousness distinct from his mind, body, personality. There is a perch free of worldly and bodily concerns. To give his attention to this indwelling presence, prostrate before his Innermost, is now his life's work..

The observant man knows the life the "I" envisions for itself is one of comfort, indulgence, and grandiosity. His warrior essence, intent on reclaiming its soul, will sacrifice these imaginings by observing them with dispassion and without identification.

His consciousness is a battlefield. The darkness offers rule of a kingdom of insatiable desire, (the next drug, the next app, the next superfood, the next sensation...) The light offers self-imposed submission and continuous dying permeated with luminous love. The fact that he knows intellectually at which altar to worship makes NO difference. The observant man does not have full command of his faculties, and thus finds himself pursuing false paradises.

The observant man's laundry list of complaints, hurts and betrayals indulge his "I" and bolster his self-consideration. He has the blessing of a healthy body and the luxury to thirst for wisdom. In having the time and the notion to meditate, the Buddhists would say he "hit pay dirt." Who is he to grumble about anything? He longs for God and dies to his grievances.

"Transcendent wisdom is inexpressible, inconceivable, unborn, unceasing and has the nature of emptiness."

The Buddha Shakyamuni

Higher consciousness requires no particular belief and cannot be known by the intellect, the personality, the emotions or the body. Transcendence is acquired by piercing the obstacles that shroud the experience of his Innermost. The observant man patiently sits and directs his attention on the space between his thoughts, in search of an authentic Self. Here his awareness may dwell on a silence whose nectar is wisdom.

Justification has no value. The observant man need not rationalize his decisions. His intuition was either correct or not. He listened to his Being or an ego, and he takes ownership of the consequences.

If the observant man really understood that he- the "I," his persona, was going to die, would BE NO MORE, and if he really comprehended that the afterlife without a soul in command is a confusing proposition, then there would be no time to waste. The hero understands how precious this human life is and throws himself headlong into birth (scientific chastity,) death (comprehending and eliminating egos) and sacrifice (serving God in others.)
Heaven requires mastery.

The observant man knows that God occupies the empty and does not mingle with vanity, pride, lust, etc. If his experience is not of a superior reality, if he is not in dialogue with the higher beings, then he is still occupied by the enemy and he must pray for more assistance.

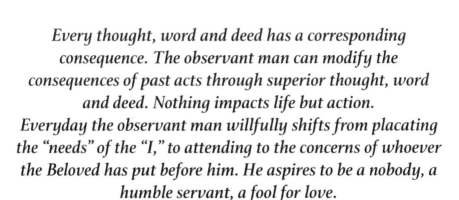

Every thought, word and deed has a corresponding consequence. The observant man can modify the consequences of past acts through superior thought, word and deed. Nothing impacts life but action.
Everyday the observant man willfully shifts from placating the "needs" of the "I," to attending to the concerns of whoever the Beloved has put before him. He aspires to be a nobody, a humble servant, a fool for love.

The observant man has encountered states free from the constraints of the "I." Samadhi, this taste of the Self unmodified, is an indescribable state of awe and freedom. To return to "normal" waking consciousness can be a disheartening separation, but the memory of this non-dualistic illumination fuels his faith and his perseverance to the path.

The observant man need not believe in Hell, it is leaking out of his interior all over his life, feeding his nightmares, fantasies, fears and vices. And as the inner God, the Being, is the soul's ticket to the cosmic God, so one's inner demons are the soul's passport to the infernal worlds. He is surprised that in this overly rational 21st century, he is motivated by avoiding a prolonged encounter with the abyss.

The observant man believes in angels, fairies, gnomes and reincarnation. These are beliefs because he can not confirm them with his experience. Faith, on the other hand, is confidence in his experience produced by his continuity of practice: chastity, meditation and ethics- the actions that have granted him a taste of an indwelling consciousness unconstrained by time and space.

Everyday the intimate Christ inspires the observant man to demonstrate bold acts of kindness. His inner mob (laziness, doubt, comfort, resignation...) always calls for the crucifixion of his inner master, and for the release of his Barabbas (self-consideration.) He must understand that in every moment, love is on trial and the horde wants blood.

Love is the instructor, and the world is where his adoration is tested. In every moment the observant man aspires to kneel, defeat his pride, and serve everyone in order to retrieve his soul from the rebellion of I, me, mine.

For the observant man, loving God above all else is being love above all else. Being love above all else is being fully present and engaged in what one is perceiving, while simultaneously being a request to serve.

In Christianity, we are told that God loves us without conditions. In New Age psychology, we are taught to love ourselves. Which self does God love, and which self are we to adore exactly? To love the ego is to increase desire, suffering and distraction. To love the personality is to invest in a specter that decays with the body. The observant man loves his soul, his warrior will, that bears witness to his chains and longs for freedom.

As above so below, as below so above. Consider that any father and the Father's first priority is to have his children close to him. The observant man's primary concern is the same, to be obedient to his Father's will.

"Lay not up for yourselves treasures upon the earth where the moth and rust doth corrupt."

Matthew 6:19 makes clear the lunacy of investing one's attention on accumulating stuff or admiration.
The observant man's real equity is in what he can take with him at bodily death- his consciousness (his hold on love's indwelling presence.) This is his most cherished asset.

Why is the sensation of praise so desirable? As the observant man examines this question, he sees that admiration feeds his "I," making it more real and thus his awareness of the Being more distant. The Being cannot be known by the senses, it is the anti-sensation, an all-pervading cognizant love silently aware of itself.

We feed our egos through a steady diet of distraction, entertainment, useless information, the news, sports, conspiracy theories, worry, fantasy, and craving the next sensation. We nurture our soul by weaning ourselves from distractions, sitting quietly, and placing our awareness on the presence of our Innermost. The observant man builds his muscle in just "being with" his interior landscape. With composure, he sits with the legion of forces that tempt him to the past or future; he watches the "I" with its swirl of propositions and waits patiently for the eternal presence to arise in his experience.

The observant man understands that it takes a tremendous amount of energy to marshal his will, concentration and watchfulness to defeat the enemy. The conservation of his energy is paramount. While continent with his sexual energy, he is also frugal with his attention. He is careful not to squander his only true possession on sensation hopping (gossip, social media, shopping, a mint...) to placate the whims of an endless procession of egos.

The observant man knows real sacrifice must confront his ego of self-consideration. His offering must accost his attachment (money, time, pride, comfort) in order to weaken his grip on impermanence.

The observant man used to practice pink spirituality. This means that he denied the existence of the shadow and covered it with fluffy frosting such as, "Everything is perfect and part of a Divine plan," and "There are no mistakes." He believed his evolution and liberation were a forgone conclusion. In refusing to recognize his inner hell realms and the impermanence of his personality, he maintained the amnesia of his comfort zone and avoided the terror of mystical death- the demise of the "I." Now, he patiently sits and observes the layers of opacity and illusion that obscure his authentic nature- the Being. This is how he dispels the darkness.

The observant man knows someday he must relinquish his will completely. In the meantime, he uses his discipline to develop virtue, tame his mind and nurture an urgent devotion to prostrate at the feet of the Beloved.

You can't surrender what you do not possess. Through the practices- meditation, prayer, pranayama, self-observation and sacrifice, the observant man's will incrementally takes dominion over his body, mind, emotions, and sexual energy. With his soul finally in command, only then can he consider the gift of authentic submission.

"All life turns on this law of sacrifice, called the wheel of yajna. Those who veer from this and seek instead to indulge the senses for personal gratification and ignore the needs of others, live in vain and squander their life. Why did I, the Creator, set this in motion? Because this world is a learning ground, a place to discipline, train, and elevate all beings. If we decline to learn we cannot derive the benefit of the schooling."

-Bhagavad Gita

With his sermons titled as listed below:

WE ARE ALL ASLEEP AND
WE ARE ASLEEP TO BEING ASLEEP.

SEX IS SACRED,
BUT ORGASMS ARE COSTLY.

HELL IS LIKELY, BUT NOT FOREVER.

95% OF WHAT YOU THINK, FEEL, SAY AND
EXPERIENCE IS CURATED
BY THE ENEMY.

LOVE WITHOUT SACRIFICE IS
SOMETHING ELSE.

HEAVEN IS A CONQUEST.

FOR MANY ARE CALLED BUT FEW
(VERY FEW) ARE CHOSEN.

GOD DOESN'T CARE
WHAT YOU BELIEVE.

*it is no surprise the observant man's church
is sparsely attended.*

Lord Derby's Pew, Knowsley Church 1869. Illustrated London News

The "I" is insistent on shaping its world with a plethora of opinions, theories, lofty ideas and remarks that all thirst for validation and promote its self- importance. These desperate projections birthed of ignorance obscure reality. More and more the observant man practices being receptive, perceiving the world from the calm abiding of his soul. In cherished moments he experiences a glimpse of his consciousness as an instrument of the Beloved, created so the One Presence could gaze upon, praise upon, it's Self.

The consciousness perceives and the mind interprets through comparison. Transcendent wisdom has no opposite; it is experienced in infinite degrees of expanding awareness, so it remains out of the intellect's reach. When the observant man notices the unsolicited commentary of his intellect, he is reminded to retrieve his awareness by watching this internal dialogue with dispassion. He is grateful for his intelligence, a useful servant but a Godless master.

The path is first human, then Divine. Impeccable virtue is a pre-condition for the veil to lift, as the Lord does not enter a defiled temple. The observant man knows he must first develop an immaculate heart without pride or lust, and a love of service before he is granted access to the superior realms.

It is simple, but not easy. First, what the observant man must do is manage his unconsciousness- his forgetting, his amnesia, his pride and desire.

The unconsciousness of others triggers the unconsciousness in him and vise versa. Around he goes distracted, defensive and sleepwalking on the wheel of Samsara. Being observant is breaking this cycle, incarnating cognizant love at all costs, being vigilant about minding his mind, sobering up from the intoxication of materialism and getting authentic about how much suffering he bears. He nurtures virtue, gets on his knees and asks for deliverance.

He must create an alliance with his Innermost and die to all propositions other than waking up. He uses his sexual energy to anoint his subtle senses, starves his demons with acts of kindness and service, and masters meditation. In silence he distinguishes the voice of his Being from that of his legion and surrenders to those instructions. He is honored, humbled and moved to have found the path home, all the while knowing that he will be severely tested. He knows that pride and lust are lurking, ready to take him down; he is vulnerable.

Within him, the Being sits serenely in adoration of the Lord. His infant soul longs to prostrate before the Being, but his feeble worship power is drawn out into the dream of his identity by the grandiosity of the "I." The observant man's consciousness is seduced by the promise of admiration and endless sensation. In every moment lives this choice: feed the will of an ego by acting upon a desire, or remember that what one is really wanting, wants our attention and abides within.

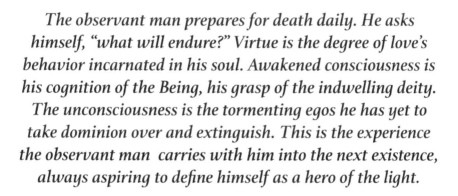

The observant man prepares for death daily. He asks himself, "what will endure?" Virtue is the degree of love's behavior incarnated in his soul. Awakened consciousness is his cognition of the Being, his grasp of the indwelling deity. The unconsciousness is the tormenting egos he has yet to take dominion over and extinguish. This is the experience the observant man carries with him into the next existence, always aspiring to define himself as a hero of the light.

POETRY

IF THE DOORS OF
PERCEPTION WERE
CLEANSED EVERYTHING
WOULD APPEAR TO MAN AS
IT IS, INFINITE.
-William Blake

On my knees is the beginning of wisdom.
Inflated and upright proves to be a sham.
I like it down here, prostate before
Love's consorted effort
To coordinate
A myriad of luminous guides
With outstretched arms,
Leading this stray dog
To the dignity from which he fell.

History suggests that all occupied people
Engage in resistance to throw off their oppressor.
Paul proposes that the only worthy enemy is within,
And to eliminate this inner assailant is called,
"The Great Work."
Assistance from outside the enemy's territory is
essential,
There are allies trying every frequency to reach you.
Our liberators advocate three essential strategies:
Kneel and die to your pride,
Nothing purifies a nest of vanities like
Martial repentance.
Tame your animal passion,
Harness and direct your creative forces
To blast your demons without mercy.
Volunteer for suffering in the service of the beloved,
Your enlistment in this egocide mission
Will obliterate the last vestiges of your self-absorption.

Own all your defects,
Defer all praise to God.
Beware of anything that nurtures the "I,"
That which builds personality,
Fortifies the enemy.
Make a career of virtue,
And be stingy in opinions,
The Beloved invites you into her arms in every
moment,
Was there something else you were chasing?
When the charm of the senses pulls you outward,
And your identity smells a conquest,
Run for your life inward,
Duck inside your heart,
Before your Innermost is shrouded in opacity.

A grateful thought drifts into a measure of one's
spiritual progress,
An act of generosity ends up searching for praise,
Toasting a friend disintegrates into jealousy,
then shame,
A truly revolutionary idea ends up fortifying a
rebellious ego,
On this knife's edge of being,
The betrayer mingles sweetly disguised,
All who enter must be examined,
This vigil is a drowning man's battle for a breath,
To retreat from this precipice,
Is to choose to slumber again,
Until our innate warrior arouses us,
To go another round.

On behalf of her son,
She always shows up at court,
And asks the judge to consider,
That he was occupied,
At the time of the infraction,
By a legion of misfits,
And asks for mercy as she displays,
An image of him before the Fall,
Her eyes see no corruption.

At the morning huddle,
The Mother is my squire,
She and I prepare to take new ground,
We go over the orders,
Conscious effort and voluntary suffering,
I sharpen my armaments,
"God is Love," "The enemy is within,"
"abstain, be silent, die,"
We map out my predictable pitfalls,
Impatience, arrogance, doubt,
Review my most enticing baits,
Billboards, stinginess, control freaks, dogma...
And then I pre-forgive all sentient beings,
For our pride in attending to all other altars,
With a rallying cry,
"Thank you God for not giving up on me,"
I alert the temple guards,
And greet another Samsaric dawn,
On the besieged ascent for home.

Having submitted to the Godhead for years,
Many petitions for total tenancy,
My legion of occupants,
Still stubbornly refuse eviction,
Leaving this son overwhelmed,
By the elaborate posturing of their representative,
A shyster, ceaselessly scamming for an audience,
In the temple of my heart.

To terminate this psychosis,
Today's strategy is a siege,
Starve out the enemy,
Put an end to this tedium of sensation hopping,
A mint, a coffee, check my phone, a trivial fantasy, ahhh!.....
With no dominion of mind,
I risk the boredom of waiting out the static
Squirming to the sting,
Of ten thousand cravings,
Renouncing all other suitors
Fractured and kneeling before,
My true reality,
Patiently still,
Giving Her a clear shot,
At the underbelly of my fraudulence.

Into my creative center,
the Mother keeps depositing cab fare home,
I squander this Spiritual capital,
On rides into neighborhoods of greater opacity,
The memory of her welcome, her guidance, her
unfailing devotion,
Slips into obscurity as the company I keep is cruder still.
Soon her payment will be of an unknown origin,
And I'll refer to some authority lacking serpentine
credentials to be soothing and comfort my
undiagnosed amnesia.

PRAYERS AND EXERCISES

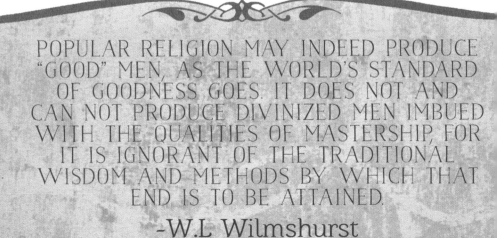

POPULAR RELIGION MAY INDEED PRODUCE
"GOOD" MEN, AS THE WORLD'S STANDARD
OF GOODNESS GOES. IT DOES NOT AND
CAN NOT PRODUCE DIVINIZED MEN IMBUED
WITH THE QUALITIES OF MASTERSHIP, FOR
IT IS IGNORANT OF THE TRADITIONAL
WISDOM AND METHODS BY WHICH THAT
END IS TO BE ATTAINED.

-W.L Wilmshurst

PRAYER FOR SPIRITUAL PROTECTION:

Klim Krishnaya Govindaya Gopijana Vallabhaya Swaha
(Make the Microcosmic Star while you say out loud)
May the power of Love protect me

Klim Krishnaya Govindaya Gopijana Vallabhaya Swaha
(Make the Microcosmic Star while you say out loud)
May the power of Love guide me

Klim Krishnaya Govindaya Gopijana Vallabhaya Swaha
(Make the Microcosmic Star while you say out loud)
May the power of Love illuminate me

Klim Krishnaya Govindaya Gopijana Vallabhaya Swaha

MORNING PRAYER:

Internal Mother,
Internal Father,
Intimate Christ,
My Being,
My Innermost,
This is the consciousness, the essence, imprisoned in ego,
fully identified with a body and a personality.
I am bowing before you, acknowledging you as my inner
master, my way home, my true reality.
Thank you for another day of listening and being guided,
Thank you for another day of vigilant self-observation
and self-remembrance,
Thank you for another day to perform the Great Work,
Thank you for another day of mystical death
and meditation,
Thank you another day of scientific chastity,
Thank you for another day in service to God and humanity,
Thank you for another day of incarnating the love of
the Father,
Thank you for another day of putting God above all things,
Thank you for another day of nurturing and
developing virtue,
Thank you for another day of dying to any ambition
other than merging with the Beloved.
May I remember God with every breath today.
Today I am asking for: permission, guidance,
healing, revelation..._____

THE RUNE FA
(To infuse the body with the Solar forces)

---

*Today I am asking permission to ascend the seven steps and enter the
Temple of the Runes.*

*(Acknowledge the two columns of the Temple Jachin
(white/masculine) and Boaz (black/feminine))*

and receive the teaching of the FAAAAAAA.

*(Extend your arms and face the palms of your hands towards the sun
(or towards the east,) left hand held a little higher than the right.
While chanting the mantras below out loud, imagine the sun's
energy being absorbed through your hands, going down your arms
into the base of your spine and then rising from the coccyx
to the corresponding chakra. Repeat 3x.)*

*Marvelous forces of love, revive my sacred fires so that my
consciousness may awaken.*

FAAAAAAAAAAAAA (lungs)
FAAAAAAYYYYYYY (throat)
FEEEEEEEEEEEEEE (crown and third eye)
FOOOOOOOOOOO (heart)
FUUUUUUUUUUU (solar plexus)

(Give thanks after three repetitions.)

*Solar hero Wodin, thank you for the teachings of the Runes.
Celestial Masters, thank you for reviving the Runes in my lifetime.
All my teachers, past, present and future, in this world and in the
superior worlds, thank you.*
*Divine Mother, thank you for rising up in me through the merits of
my heart, meeting thy Husband in my crown and birthing the Son
in my heart. Thank you.*

Artwork by Jon Marro

THE LORD'S PRAYER

Our Father who art in Heaven,
(My inner father that dwells in my pineal gland)

Hallowed be thy name,
(Your name is the sacred word:
Jehovah Elohim. הוהי. Yodd Hay Vav Hay)

Thy Kingdom come, thy will be done,
(I surrender to the guidance of my Being)

On earth as it is in Heaven,
(In my mental, emotional and creative centers)

Give us this day our daily bread,
(Please give me a taste of your experience, your bliss)

And forgive us our trespasses as we forgive those that
trespass against us,
(And forgive me when I go unconscious- forget God, as I forgive those
who go unconscious- forget God)

And lead us not into temptation, but deliver us from evil,
(Guide me in my ordeals and protect me from the tenebrous)

For thine is the power and the glory and the kingdom,
(For you are the only reality, the only truth, my heart's desire)

Forever and ever, Amen.

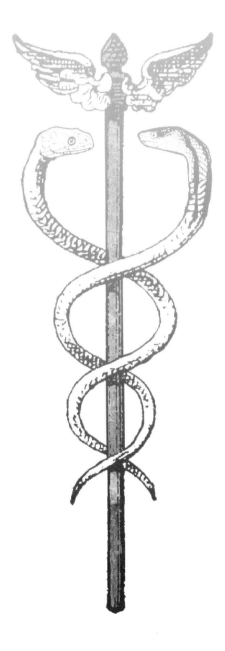

EXERCISES FOR SUBLIMATION OF THE CREATIVE/SEXUAL ENERGY.

I alternate between these two techniques to prevent the process from going mechanical. These practices are living prayers that implore the Divine Mother Kundalini (as Moses lifted the serpent in the wilderness) to transform our sexual energy and fill our temple with her light. Impeccable ethics and virtue are a prerequisite.

HAM SAA

1. Sit with your back in a comfortable upright position with your eyes closed.

2. As you inhale through your nose, imagine light moving up your spine from your coccyx to the crown of your head. As you do this inwardly (mentally), chant the mantra HAAM. (A is soft like "ah")

3. Hold your breath here for as long as you can and still stay relaxed and comfortable. (Important to be relaxed)

4. Release a short burst of breath (The exhale should be shorter than the inhale) and out loud chant SSAAAAAAA. At the same time, imagine the light in the crown of your head falling over your forehead, past your throat and into your heart.

5. Repeat for 10-15 minutes before meditation.

EGYPTIAN CHRISTIC PRANAYAMA

1. Sit with your back in a comfortable, upright position with your eyes closed.

2. With your thumb and middle finger, practice closing off the right and left nostrils.

3. Women start by closing off the left nostril and inhaling through the right nostril.

Men close off the right nostril and inhale through the left nostril.

4. As you inhale, imagine a column of energy/light rising up your spine

from the coccyx to the crown of your head. At the same time, inwardly (silently) chant TOAN (like the English word tone but elongated) TOOAANNN. Contract your perineum as if you were holding your pee.

5. At the top of your breath when the light reaches the crown of your head, chant inwardly SSSSAAAA.

6. Hold your breath for at least a moment.

7. Switch nostrils. Women are exhaling through their left nostril and

men are exhaling through their right nostril while chanting inwardly HAAMMMM. Imagine the light descending from your crown over your forehead past your throat, into your heart. Release your perineum.

8. Women then inhale through their left nostril and men through their

right nostril while inwardly chanting TOOAANN. Imagine a column of light moving up the spine from the coccyx to the crown of your head. Contract your perineum.

9. At the top of your breath when the light reaches the crown of your head chant inwardly RRAAAA. (pronounced RRAAHHH)

10. Hold your breath for at least a moment.

11. Switch Nostrils and exhale (women through the right, men through

the left) while inwardly chanting HAAMMM and imagining the light descending from your crown, across your forehead past your throat, into your heart. Relax your perineum. This finishes one complete round. Repeat 9x for a full set.

PRAYER TO ACTIVATE THE CHAKRAS

(THE SENSE ORGANS THROUGH WHICH WE PERCEIVE SUPERIOR WORLDS
The Seven Churches in the Book of Revelation)

My Father, my God, Divine Goddess, Mother of mine,
Help me activate the 7 vowels,
So that Johannes, the Word of God,
Will prepare my body for the advent of the word,
Jesus in my heart.

Eeee, eeee...
(Third eye)

Aayyyyyyy...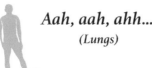
(Throat)

Ohh, ohh, ohh...
(Heart)

Uuuuu...
(Solar plexus)

Aah, aah, ahh...
(Lungs)

Mmm, mmm,mmm...
(Prostate/Uterus)

Ssssssss...
(Creative organs)

A PRAYER FOR SEXUAL REDEMPTION

Pronounce the mantra Ramm- Eeeeeee- Ooooo 3x

Dear Mother,
With great remorse and regret I recall my trespasses.
I have squandered my spiritual capital,
I have spilled my sexual energy,
I have blasphemed the Holy Spirit,
I have wasted precious time nurturing desire
and fantasy, and lust,
I have participated in fornication, masturbation,
pornography, prostitution, adultery and abortion.
It is with bitterness and shame that I kneel before you.
Mother please be merciful,
I need your help,
Please revive my sacred fires,
So my consciousness can awaken,
Please know that I cherish my chastity and
protect it with ferocity,
Please know this son is coming home.

Pronounce the mantra Ramm- Eeeeeee- Ooooo 3x

PRAYER FOR COOPERATION WITH THE ELEMENTALS OF NATURE

Elemental Advocate, the part of my Being that communicates with the elemental world.
Please on my behalf thank the Undines, Sylphs, Salamanders, Gnomes, Deva's and Nature Spirits that operate here in the environs of Be Love Farm for their perfect work.

I don't see you, but I see the results of your efforts and am grateful.

Please ask them to try and pierce my density and communicate with me through inspiration and intuition, so that we together can make a jewel of creation here at Be Love Farm.

I am at your service.

Thank you.

PRAYER TO THE DIVINE MOTHER FOR ELIMINATION OF EGOS:

Dear Mother,
Please consider my petitions,
Please deliver me to the feet of Lord Shiva, the Holy Spirit
And beg him, implore him on my behalf
To remove, extract from me any obstacles to my
self-realization.

Please ask him to remove from me any egos, demons,
defects, psychological aggregates, habits, vices, wounds, and
sins.

Ask him to remove:
(whatever egos you have recently seen occupying you that have caused suffering)

And cast them into the inferno of my solar plexus and burn
them into cosmic dust.
(put your attention on the fire of your solar will in the solar plexus,
imagine 3x those egos being delivered and incinerated)

Thank you Mother for your understanding, your guidance,
your mercy, for not giving up on me.

Please know that this son is coming home.

I perform this prayer in Viparita Karani Mudra

PRAYER FOR THE MODIFICATION OF KARMA

Anubis, Lords of Karma, attendants of the Hall of Justice and the Temple of the Law,
Please hear my praises and consider my petitions,
This spark of consciousness trapped in physicality, the senses, and a legion of defects,
Would like to praise you for the patient, merciful service that you provide,
For this dense degenerating humanity.
Eon after eon you are there for us to strategize for our best development,
And lifetime after lifetime we return to you having fallen and failed to advance with repeated mistakes,
And without judgement, and with only our soul's redemption in mind you send us on our way again,
Your service is Divine love in action, thank you.
I have a few petitions, I may not have the karmic equity to pay for these petitions,
If this is so, let me know how I can serve, how I can sacrifice to pay for these petitions.

EXAMPLE OF PETITIONS

1. Please grant me a long and healthy life in this body so I can continue working with the three jewels and meditation.
2. In my next life may I be born into a family that practices and teaches mystical death, sexual alchemy, service to God and humanity, and meditation, so I can get an early start.
3. Please help Carol with her health challenge and if appropriate, use some of my karmic equity to heal her.

Thank you for your consideration. If my prayer has in any way been lacking humility, please forgive me. I know the lion of the law is won on the scales.

Follow with the mantra: Neeee, Naaaay, Nooooo, Nuuuuu, Naaah- 3X.

PRAYER BEFORE MEDITATION

Internal Mother, Internal Father, Intimate Christ,
my Being, my Innermost,
Please take full tenancy of my consciousness,
I invite you to evict my "I's," my egos.
Throw out the money changers,
Occupy me,
Arise in my awareness,
As my true identity.

MEDITATION

❧

The Kingdom of Heaven is within. The physical senses only perceive the most basic level of creation (the outer physical) so we must withdraw from them to access higher realms. When we withdraw inward we find psychological chaos. We have to bring order to our "wilderness." Meditation is the fundamental tool for distinguishing consciousness from the mind and all that distracts us. Without accessing our indwelling silence, how can we distinguish the false propositions of the ego from the song of our Innermost? From this stillness we can clearly see our defects and take dominion over our three brains (intellect, emotions, sexual/ motor/instinctual.) This is how we possess our soul so the Lord can begin to enter our experience. To achieve this kind of purity without a meditation practice I suggest is impossible. Make it your daily bread. For training I recommend the Meditation Essentials course on **gnosticteachings.org***. It is free to download.*

CONSIDERATIONS FOR DEVELOPING
A SPIRITUAL DIARY

THERE IS A TREASURY OF
JOY WITHIN YOU,
WHY DO YOU KEEPING
BEGGING DOOR TO DOOR?
-Rumi

MORNING PRACTICES

**Dream Journal —
Did you remember your
dreams?**

Prayers_____

Sublimation of sexual energy_____

Runes_____

**Upon waking, what mood,
emotional experience were you
in? Any idea why?**

Minutes of Meditation? _____

DURING THE DAY
YOUR REMEMBRANCE MENU IN THE THROES OF THE BATTLE:

Abstain, be silent and die.

If you are confronted, close your eyes and take a deep breath before you speak.

Before you speak, ask yourself these questions:

Is it true?
Is it kind?
Is it useful?
Is it necessary?

The challenging people in your life are your Zen Masters, training you in staying present, seated in love. Their upset is your meditation.

Ask yourself, "What would love do now?"

Forgive them Father, for they know not what they do. (Include yourself in the "they.")

Three questions to ask yourself throughout the day:

Who is having this experience?

Where do I think this experience is located?

What is the purpose of this experience?

Ask yourself and others what they are grateful for.

Remember, you are the awareness that is watching your thoughts, emotions, and actions arise.

Love everyone
Serve everyone
Remember your Being.

DAY IN REVIEW BEFORE BED

Did you acknowledge or recognize your Innermost as your true reality?

Did you speak from vanity?

Did you gossip, diminish, criticize, or complain?

Did you keep your chastity?

How well did you serve others?

Did you give thanks before you ate?

Did you waste time and energy with useless chatter or activities?

Did you identify any new or persistent egos?

Did you petition the Divine Mother to eliminate any egos?

Did lust make an appearance today?

How did pride infect your day?

What other vices were you conscious of today?

What mechanical or habitual behavior did you observe today?

What negative emotions appeared today?

In what ways were you stingy with love?

Did you get seduced by money today?

What was today's biggest distraction?

What was today's greatest victory?

What instructions or downloads did you receive from your Innermost?

What did you crave today?

What did you sacrifice?

EVENING PRACTICES BEFORE BED

Prayers_____

Sublimation of sexual energy_____

Minutes of Meditation _____

SACRIFICE
SACRED OFFICE, HOLY OFFERING

INRI.

Igne Natura Renovatur Integra. Fire Renews Nature Incessantly.

This acronym hangs above the crucified Jesus to remind us that sacrifice is the key to restoration and spiritual progression. Consider that how we restore our lives is through sacrifice. In the Great Work, we sacrifice our vices, the sexual spasm and our own comfort and consideration to serve God and others. The natural world is a perfect demonstration of the renewal of life through this process. Each generation of life sacrifices itself for the next. Nature is a complex regenerating system that is constantly devouring itself for revival. Watch any documentary on a watering hole in Africa to see this Christic principle in action. Predation, volcanoes, forest fires, floods, compost heaps, winters, droughts and flood all bring renewal. Annual plants sacrifice their body to produce the seed. Pruning trees invigorates them.

How we renew any relationship is through the sacrifice of apology or forgiveness. Both require the death of egoic pride. Great leaders make sacrifices to communities and organizations to renew their inspiration or mission. Gandhi's famous fast for peace between Muslims and Hindus comes to mind. We renew our spiritual lives through sacrifice, because when we live for the other and die to our self-consideration, we make room in our hearts for Christ (the consciousness of Love) to enter. God cannot fill what is already full.

To keep one's sacrifice from drifting to martyrdom or pride, (poor me, I work harder, I am more humble) or becoming narcissistic, (only experienced internally, "I gave up bad thoughts about my mother") one must be diligent that the sacrifice has both an external and internal action. External action must live in the world and requires the giving up of our agenda, time, resources, money, comfort, energy, etc. Internal action means we sacrifice any corresponding egos connected to that external sacrifice. Any realized expectations or defects must be dominated or eliminated (I am generous, is anyone looking, Holier than thou, God loves me because I...) Giving anonymously when possible is a way to help manage the "I'm good" ego. We must give up the admiration that bolsters the "I" for blossoming, luminous love of our Being.

To renew our spiritual life, we express love for its own sake. Love is honed on the stone of sacrifice. We must fall on the sword of humility again and again and defeat our selfishness in the service of others. There is no greater sacrifice than giving up the life our "I" imagines for us. This is how we renew our grip on the path and allow the experience of our Being to unfold in our consciousness. We can always be looking for the opportunity to serve others at the expense of our cravings and comforts. This is the Sacred Office of those who aspire to die and be reborn. Delighting others or relieving their suffering is the path of our aliveness. Trying to satisfy our own endless parade of desires does nothing but cement us deeper in ignorance. Everyday the observant man looks for where to be love, abate suffering, crush his inner legion, and live in freedom. The bonus is that another, at least for a moment, may be extracted from scarcity and aloneness.

I have a cause.
We need those don't we?
Otherwise the darkness and cold gets in and everything
starts to ache.
My soul has a purpose, it is to love;
if I do not fulfill my hearts vocation,
I suffer.

-Thomas Aquinas

CLARIFICATION OF TERMS

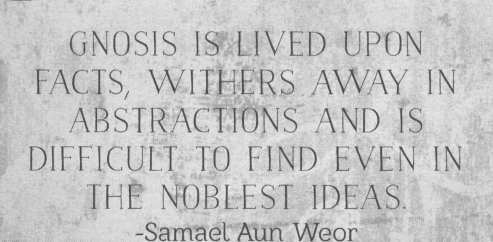

GNOSIS IS LIVED UPON
FACTS, WITHERS AWAY IN
ABSTRACTIONS AND IS
DIFFICULT TO FIND EVEN IN
THE NOBLEST IDEAS.
-Samael Aun Weor

The Being

The Being is our personal Deity, our internal Mother, Father and Intimate Christ. It is our individual Trinity, our Innermost. The Being is the part of the Divine that followed us into matter but did not fall. The Being orbits just outside the awareness of our contaminated consciousness. It is our coach and inner Master guiding our soul through our intuition and inspiration to develop and defeat the darkness.
The Being needs our fallen consciousness to join with it, so that in union it can return to the cosmic Father. Ethics, meditation and the three jewels (mystical death, scientific chastity, and service to God and humanity) are how we incarnate our Being.

Christ

Christ is the Alpha and Omega. The purpose and final outcome of creation is to know Christ. Christ is a part of the Cosmic Trinity and our internal Trinity. Christ is an exalted state of consciousness, a title, a cosmic rank. Christ is birthed in our experience when the Divine Mother (Holy Spirit) rises up our spine ("and as Moses lifted up the serpent in the wilderness." John 3:14.) into the pineal gland where our internal Father dwells, and then together they descend into our hearts where the Christ child is born. Christification for all souls is the goal of creation. Jesus incarnated the Christ and is the most celebrated of masters, the king of many historical Christs. The Gospels are a road map for all of us to enter the path of initiation and perform the Great Work.

Comprehension of an ego

Our consciousness/essence is mostly trapped in craving or aversion, with brief and rare moments of freedom which might be experienced as love, peace, or bliss. We must comprehend our imprisoning defects distinct from that which perceives, our essence, and then offer this foreign entity up to a higher power to eliminate. God will not destroy that which we perceive as "I." What is our Divine Mother going to take aim at if we experience the ego as our self? In meditation we establish a foundation of silence whereupon we can experience the perceiver (our essence) as distinct from that which it identifies with. Once we can see that it is our attention that gets hypnotized by a particular ego, we can also see the suffering it causes. Until we comprehend the cost of identifying with a particular ego, we are unlikely to be motivated to stop feeding it. Once we experience the ego as distinct from our consciousness and are remorseful for the pain it creates, then we can offer up this cleverly disguised defect and pray for its elimination.

Divine Mother

How can there be a Father without a Mother? The Divine Mother is the feminine aspect of God. She is our intimate, internal Deity as well as a cosmic Deity. In many traditions, it is she that is called upon to destroy our egos. She never abandons her children and lies hidden in our base chakra (represented by Mary, always at the base of the cross) ready to awaken through the merits of our heart. She goes by many names- Isis, Aphrodite, Devi Kundalini, Mary, Kali. She is the Pentecostal fire that unleashes herself up though our spine to open our spiritual sight as we learn ethical behavior and use our sexual energy for self-realization.

Ego

Ego is a rebellion, a virus named "I" that rejects God above all else. The multiplicity of contradictory psychological elements, the conjunction of competing wills that we have inside are the sum of "ego." Every ego is a defect that causes suffering and distracts us from God in our heart. The seven deadly sins, our vices, fears, neuroses, demons, "the mind," and all their variants are egos. In Buddhism, 84,000 are mentioned. In the Bhagavad Gita, Arjuna faces a vast army of enemy relatives; these are his egos. This is the inner mob that demands the crucifixion (wants to negate the experience) of the Intimate Christ, demonstrated externally 2,000 years ago and more importantly, daily, in our internal world.

Essence

Essence and consciousness are the same, the spark of Divine light bottled up in egoic modification. Essence is the fledgling soul trapped in desire but assigned to incarnate superior consciousness. As the observant man eliminates a defect and develops virtue, more essence is freed or more soul is possessed.

Gnosis

Knowledge or wisdom that has been acquired through direct experience. Gnosis cannot be gained by belief or the intellect. The description of the flavor of an orange can only be verified or understood by the eating of an orange. This is gnosis of an orange.

Gnostic

A person who pursues Gnosis, the direct perception of truth.

God, The Beloved, The Divine, The Trinity

Elohim, the word for God in Genesis means Gods and Goddesses. God is a Multi-Unity, a myriad of beings that serve the one common will of Christ, love and wisdom. What we long to experience or return to is this state of consciousness from which we came. Nothing else will quench our eternal thirst. This mystery that the mind and senses cannot know is our quest, first by incarnating our inner God, the Being, which will then lead us to the Cosmic God.

The Great Work

The Great Work refers to the progression of consciousness towards Christification, or the soul merging with the consciousness of Christ. This is achieved through the three jewels- mystical death (Sanctity), sexual alchemy (Chastity), and service and sacrifice for God and humanity (Charity).

Hell

Hell is a psychological state of inner torment created by our egos, as well as a denser plane of existence than this physical world. Hell is mentioned in nearly all religious traditions. If the human being cannot liberate his/her soul from the ego after multiple opportunities (108 incarnations are mentioned in Buddhism,) then the compassionate system of the Divine will cleanse the infected consciousness through the levels of hell (9 are mentioned by Dante) to give the essence a clean start, a return to innocence. For the ego, hell is in a sense eternal damnation, but not for the soul.

Karma

Karma is the law of cause and effect; "As you sow, so shall you reap." Similar to Newton's third law, "For every action there is an equal and opposite reaction," karma is the consequence of any action returning to the soul that performed the action. If one steals, the law of karma assures that that soul will experience being robbed. If one is generous, then one will know the charity of others. Karma is a law to educate the soul on the impact of its actions. Like the law of gravity, it applies to all. Karma responds to all actions without discrimination and reciprocates. It not a system of reward and punishment based on morality.

Four principles of karma:
1. All actions (thoughts, words, deeds) have a consequence.
2. The consequence is greater than the action that caused it.
3. You cannot receive the consequence without committing the corresponding action.
4. The consequence can be amended or annulled through a superior action but can never be erased.

Mystical Death

This is the process of ego elimination. One identifies the particular ego, vice, habit, neurosis, demon, and then contemplates its nature and the suffering it creates. Next, one must comprehend it as a separate entity from one's essence (that which perceives) and then one prays to a higher power to eliminate it. This is how we gradually take back our soul.

Pranayama

Harnessing our vital and sexual energy through breathing exercises, often in preparation for meditation.

Samsara

The cycle of birth and death to which material life is bound.

Sexual Magic, Scientific Chastity, Sexual Priesthood, White Tantra

Consider that our sexual energy is the most powerful force within us. It has within it the potency to create new life and also the capability to anoint our spiritual ascension or our spiritual degradation. Sexual energy unmanaged drives humans to betray all standards of morality. What would have a man violate his daughter but a very potent energy in the hands a maniacal force called the ego? This is why all spiritual traditions put in structures to guide and harness our sexual forces.
The sexual energy is the creative power of the Holy Spirit. Sexual magic refers to directing this force up the spine to the crown of our head to open and develop our spiritual senses. For a single person, this means sublimating the sexual force with various exercises (see practices.) For committed couples, it refers to sexual intercourse, also directing the energy upward while refraining from the orgasm. The couple retains the very charged energy field that only a couple can create and they use that power to kill desire and nurture adoration for the Beloved. In both cases, this is symbolized in scripture as having one's head anointed with oil. The preserved energy is utilized to develop concentration and willpower, eliminate egos and build one's solar body (this is the wedding garment mentioned in Matthew 22:12) with which one can live in the superior worlds. This is the second birth referred to in the Gospels.

Our culture is sexually degenerated. Lust is never fulfilled, it only wants more, different, extreme. Traditional sexuality within the container of a committed, loving marriage often loses the passion and luster because the ego of lust is insatiable. These relationships often degrade to indifference, adultery (fantasized or acted upon,) pornography use, etc. Look how much pain irresponsible sexual relations cause. It is not a stretch to imagine that we use sex for the wrong reasons- mostly carnal pleasure and procreation occasionally. Rather than expending it, imagine if one retained all the highly charged sexual energy that one had engendered in a lifetime, and used it to take dominion over one's three brains (mental, emotional, motor/sexual/instinctual.) But there is nothing to believe in here, you can verify this for yourself. Consider the challenge of being continent with your sexual energy (refrain from having orgasms) and practice the sublimation exercises in the prayers section of this book everyday for 90 days. You can validate for yourself whether you have more dominion over your mind(s) and egos. I assert that your ability to bear witness, be observant, and stay present will be amplified.

As a farmer, it makes no sense to plant seed where I have no interest in growing a crop. I don't expend seed without purpose, that would drain my energy. When we expel our sexual energy, we are trading the possibility of eternity for a momentary sensation. Notice how our corrupted culture, with almost every message, manipulates us through the promise of sensation (sex sells.) The media constantly entices us to release our sexual energy which keeps us spiritually blind and bound to Samsara.

Jesus's ministry started at a wedding, as does ours. How we turn the water (animal sexuality) into the wine of the Lord is to channel our greatest power for God realization. Adoring our partner and the Divine while retaining our sexual energy is the ultimate exercise in "deny thyself." To walk through the sexual fire and not get burned (release) is a supreme example of mastery over the enemy- desire.

References to Sexual Magic

The generative energy, which, when we are loose, dissipates and makes us unclean. When we are continent, it invigorates and inspires us. Chastity is the flowering of man; and what are called Genius, Heroism, Holiness and the like are but various fruits which succeed it.
-Henry David Thoreau, Walden

If the Veerya (sexual energy) is lost through orgasm, Prana gets unsteady. Prana is agitated. The man becomes nervous. Then the mind also can't work properly. The man becomes fickle-minded. There is mental weakness. If the Prana is rendered steady, the mind becomes steady. If the Veerya (sexual energy) is steady, the mind is also steady. Veerya is the essence of life, thought, intelligence and consciousness. Therefore, preserve this vital fluid very, very carefully.
-Swami Sivananda

*Veerya is the root of the words virile and virtue.

Being able to have sexual contact without releasing the semen is something needed when you practice the advanced stages of the complete stage.
-The 14th Dalai Lama (Berzin Archives)

When the precious jewel of semen is mastered, anything on earth can be mastered.
Through the grace of its preservation, one becomes as great as me
(Shiva.) Knowing this the yogi must always preserve the semen*.
This is the ultimate Yoga.
-Shiva Samita
*Semen is referring to male and female sexual energy

*Whoever has been born of God does not sin, for His seed remains in him; and he cannot
sin, because he has been born of God.*
1 John 3:9

**The following Old Testament verse is referred to by Jesus in the New Testament
(below) on the results of the two kinds of sexuality. One brings spiritual life and the
other spiritual death.**

*And the people spake against God, and against Moses, "Wherefore have ye brought us up
out of Egypt to die in the wilderness? For there is no bread, neither is there water; and our
soul loatheth this light bread." And the Lord sent fiery serpents among the people, and they
bit the people; and many people of Israel died. Therefore the people came to Moses, and
said, "We have sinned, for we have spoken against the Lord and against thee; pray unto
the Lord that he take away the serpents from us." And Moses prayed for the people. And
the Lord said unto Moses, "Make thee a fiery serpent and set it upon a pole: and it shall
come to pass that everyone that is bitten, when they look upon it, shall live." And Moses
made a serpent of brass, and put it on a pole, and it came to pass, that if a serpent had
bitten a man, when he beheld the serpent of brass, he lived.*
-Numbers 21

And as Moses lifted up the serpent in the wilderness, even so must the Son of man be lifted up.
John 3:14

יהשוה

Yeshua, Jesus, the Christ.

In Hebrew when you put the letter ש Shin, fire, or the Christ in the midst of the letters for man and the woman, you spell the word Yeshua or Jehoshua, which indicates Jesus, the Savior. Through sexual union, through sexual cooperation, through the mastery of sexual fire, the savior is born.

Soul

"In your patience possess ye your soul." **Luke 21:19**

The soul is the consciousness, or essence, which has been significantly purged of the "I" and experiences the Being as its identity. A person with a soul has significant dominion over their impulses- mental, emotional, sexual/instinctual. To have a soul is to possess a level of spiritual maturity.

The Three Brains

Consider we actually have three brains or centers of consciousness to manage, take dominion over and bring into balance. If imbalanced they can rob each other of energy. Ex. Overthinking, rampant mental chatter, will pilfer energy from the heart and body.

1. Mental- our thoughts, intellect.
2. Emotions- the watery world of our emotions.
3. Motor/instinctual/ sexual- our urges and impulses.

Yoga

Religion comes from the Latin "religare" meaning, "to bind" (to God.) Similarly, Yoga means union. It is a science of union with our Being. Yoga has eight progressive steps; a version of this progression exists in most spiritual lineages. While the steps can be engaged simultaneously, they cannot be skipped. One cannot expect to be relaxed in their body or have a still mind if one's behavior is unethical. Similarly, if one is incontinent with their sexual energy, it is unlikely they will be able to keep the mind steady enough to withdraw from the senses and be fully absorbed in the ecstatic. The steps build towards the final goal of Samadhi, a state of bliss free of the constraints of the ego and in union with one's Being. At this point the devotee can receive unadulterated instructions from the Divine source. Yoga practitioners in the west often neglect steps 1&2, become obsessed with 3, making access to steps 5-8 unlikely.

1. Yama: Self-restraint — ethics; do not steal, murder, cheat, drink, lie, etc.
2. Niyama: Precepts — virtue, sexual purity, joyfully accept your karma, service to others, generosity, worship, integrity, kindness, humility…
3. Asana: Posture — relaxation, lack of agitation in the body, preparing the body to relax to such a state that the consciousness is not bound by it. Not acrobatics!
4. Pranayama: Harnessing of life force, the sexual energy, through breathing exercises.
5. Pratyahara: Suspension of senses, withdrawing from the world of form.
6. Dharana: Concentration, one-pointed focus.
7. Dhyana: Meditation — absorption in the experience of withdrawing from senses and concentration.
8. Samadhi: Super-conscious state, blissfulness, ecstasy, reality where wisdom, direct perception of Divinity can be experienced without the modification of the ego.

RESOURCES

We are extremely fortunate. What was previously only revealed to those whose commitment had been severely tested, is now taught openly. This may be the first time in history that the Great Work, the path of the Three Jewels has been taught publicly. What has been articulated in most scriptures and traditions but hidden in symbols and parables is now practically explained.

*At **gnosticteachings.org** and **venerabilisopus.org** you can find an abundance of resources (books, podcasts, videos, lectures, courses) to support your quest for a direct perception of the Divine.*

(Thangka) with the Medicine Buddha (Bhaishajyaguru) | The Art Institute of Chicago

Made in the USA
Monee, IL
11 December 2019